QUANTUM MINISTRY

QUANTUM MINISTRY

How Pastors Can Make the Leap

by D. Randy Berkner

BEACON HILL PRESS
OF KANSAS CITY

Library of Congress Cataloging-in-Publication Data

Berkner, D. Randy, 1952-
   Quantum ministry : how pastors can make the leap / D. Randy Berkner.
     p. cm.
   Includes bibliographical references.
   ISBN-13: 978-0-8341-2302-1 (pbk.)
   ISBN-10: 0-8341-2302-9 (pbk.)
   1. Pastoral theology. I. Title.

   BV4011.3.B45 2007
   253—dc22

                                                    2006100554

10 9 8 7 6 5 4 3 2 1

Contents

Introduction

The 114 residents of Tony, Wisconsin, have recognized Jim Leonhard as a star athlete for many years. During his Flambeau High School days, "Jimmy" once struck out 19 batters with a Minnesota Twins scout in the stands. An explosive guard in basketball, he once drained 10 3-pointers in a single contest. A speedy quarterback/safety in football, he accounted for 483 yards of total offense—in the first half of one game! This hometown hero is the subject of legends and lore.

Jim Leonhard, however, flew undetected below the radar of major college football scouts. Who knows why. Perhaps they were thinking, *Can any good thing come out of tiny Tony?* At any rate, he chose to join the University of Wisconsin Badgers as a "walk-on" rather than attend a smaller school that would have gladly given him a scholarship. Leonhard's legend grew on the gridiron. As UW's free safety, he led the Big Ten Conference in interceptions twice and ranks second in Badger history with 20 picks. He became the Big Ten's all-time leader in punt return yardage. Teammates recognized Jim as their most valuable player and team captain. He was twice named First Team All-America and All-Conference. At the conclusion of his senior season, Leonhard was 1 of 12 semifinalists for the Jim Thorpe Award (given to the nation's top defensive back) and 1 of 7 semifinalists for the inaugural Lott Trophy (the first collegiate football award to recognize athletic performance and the character of a player). By the way, did I mention that Jim earned a scholarship? He has single-handedly put Tony, Wisconsin, on the map.

In so many ways, Jim Leonhard is the stereotypical kid from a small town in America's dairyland—quiet, unassuming, hardworking, and humble. This standout does not stand out in a crowd. Jim is vertically challenged in his 5'8" frame and weighs only 185 pounds. His height, however, did not keep him from winning an impromptu slam-dunk contest at the Kohl Center with moves that would have made Michael Jordan smile. His vertical jump from the standing position is 35 inches! Time and time again, Badger fans saw jumping Jim go over the top of much taller receivers to snare an interception. Three of Leonhard's pigskin picks came after he suffered a broken thumb and wrist.

Jim was No. 18 in the Badger media guide but No. 1 in the hearts of fans. And frankly, it is easy to cheer for someone who handles himself so well both on and off the field. He was truly a *student*-athlete. In light of Jim's selection to the regional Academic All-American team, it is safe to say that he hit the books as solidly as he hit opposing running backs. By all accounts, Jim is a well-balanced and well-grounded young man.

Sports taught Jim valuable life lessons about discipline, hard work, persistence, cooperation, and dedication. His education began early. At the tender age of five, Jimmy wandered out to the 3-point line during a Flambeau alumni basketball function. The preschooler sank a 3-point shot and when someone bet him that he couldn't do it again, he proved them wrong by hitting two more. It wouldn't be the last time that little Jimmy successfully met a challenge.

At the time of this writing, Jim is a backup safety for the Buffalo Bills. He continues to hone his skills with an eye toward a starting position. Here's one scouting report on him, posted just prior to the NFL draft:

Strengths: Extremely productive . . . A playmaker in the secondary with a nose for the ball . . . Smart and has great instincts . . . Good character and hard worker . . . Fast and quick . . . Good overall athletic ability . . . Also a good return man.

Weaknesses: Undersized and very short . . . Only an average tackler but gives top effort . . . Might have a limited upside in the pros because of his size.

Notes: Overachiever who was a walk-on that developed into one of the top players at his position in college football . . . Doesn't have the physical tools you look for but the kind of guy you hate to doubt.[1]

How does this undersized, very short, average tackler who doesn't have the physical tools become "extremely productive"? The scout cites Jim's intellect, speed, athletic instincts, character, and work ethic. If he weren't Catholic, Jim would be the perfect poster boy for the "Protestant work ethic."

One could argue that many equally gifted, aspiring athletes demonstrate a good work ethic with limited and disappointing results. What separates Jim Leonhard from so many others? At 5'8", how does he stand head and shoulders above the rest? I propose that the distinguishing difference is Jim's passion for maximizing his potential. An overachiever? Not really—just someone who is serious about being the best he can be.

Such stories are not limited to the sports arena. We find examples of those who want to maximize their potential in every field, including the professional ministry. Take, for example, Buddy Marston—my friend and pastor of the Salem Fields Community Church in Fredericksburg, Virginia. A native of Keezletown, Virginia (population 701), Buddy rarely darkened the doors of the church when he was growing up. He was an average student who chose to pursue a career in selling truck parts rather than attend college. Buddy and his wife, Gaye, were fun-loving, financially secure, unchurched twentysomethings when God radically transformed their lives and summoned them into pastoral service. Like the original apostles, Buddy left his "nets" (i.e., a well-paying job, security, comfort zone) to follow the Master's leading—a vocational journey that began with home courses of study, Bible college extension classes, and employment as youth pastor at his home church in Harrisonburg, Virginia.

When the Marstons joined the ministry team at our church in Woodbridge, Virginia, back in 1989, I felt as though we were adding a good Christian counselor who could sing (Gaye) but privately harbored some concerns about entrusting our 30-member youth group into Buddy's care. After all, he was common in almost every way and lacked the classic ministerial training. You know, there are some individuals who seem to, by their charismatic presence, command attention when they enter a room; Buddy isn't one of them. In fact, he could walk into a room and go unnoticed for quite a while. Within weeks, he allayed my fears and exceeded everyone's expectations. Inspired by John Maxwell to grow as a leader, Buddy loved troubled kids into the Kingdom and encouraged others to do the same. The result? An energetic group of over 100 transformed teens who loved the Lord Jesus Christ far more than pizza and Pepsi!

Upon my departure from that church, several local leaders wanted Buddy and another staff associates to become copastors of the congregation. Frankly, I was a bit relieved when the District Advisory Board refused a request to have these two unproven "rookies" lead this growing congregation of 400 plus members. Was Buddy Marston ready for such an assignment? No one will ever know. We do know, however, that he soon became pastor of a church in Fredericksburg, Virginia, and has led that congregation to phenomenal growth during the past several years. In fact, some have suggested that his church may be the fastest-growing church in our denomination. God is doing extraordinary things through this ordinary pastor! An overachiever? Not really—just someone who is serious about being the best he can be.

Columnist Anna Quindlen wrote, "Once I got a fortune cookie that said, 'To remember is to understand.' I have never forgotten it. A good judge remembers what it was like to be a lawyer. A good editor remembers what it was like to be a reporter. A good parent remembers what it was like to be a child."[2] No doubt, we would all agree that a good district superintendent remembers what it was like to be a pastor. Having served as a senior pastor for almost 28 years, I have a vivid memory of ministerial life on the front lines and an experiential understanding of the joys and frustrations that come with the fulfillment of your calling within a local church. Ah, the insight of hindsight! In response to a summons from God, we have embraced a vocation that clear thinking individuals would not take up on their own. Consider the absurdity of choosing the ministry life for its work hours or financial rewards. Even though we may experience some difficulty in articulating exactly what *the call* means, we must have a strong sense that we are in this work because God wants us to be. It may be the only thing that keeps us from breaking ranks when we face friendly fire. My attempts to define the pastorate usually include the Peace Corps slogan: "It's the toughest job you'll ever love!"

Pastors are a battered breed, evidenced by the record numbers of ministerial dropouts and many more who are "weary in well-doing."

Every pastor has memorized the scriptural admonition: "Serve the LORD with gladness" (Ps. 100:2, KJV); many are haunted by it. Of those who start out in pastoral ministry during their 20s, less than half make it to retirement; 75 percent of pastors say their self-esteem is lower now than when they first entered the ministry. There are some peculiar challenges related to the ministry that make it a uniquely demanding vocation. I will give attention to many of them in the following pages. Suffice it to say at this point, a diminishing romance for ministry is almost always linked to the gut feeling that one's efforts are not making much of a difference in people's lives. Fruitfulness is fun; fruitlessness isn't. "Burnout, brownout, dissipation of energy and commitment," says William Willimon, "are matters more of distress than stress, a lack of meaning rather than a lack of energy."[3]

Quantum Ministry is written in the prayerful hope that somehow God will speak through me to restore a greater measure of joy and meaning to your pastoral journey so that you will not just remain in your assignment but will be fully engaged and fruitful as well. I am going public with evolving ideas pondered in classrooms, prayer rooms, and offices. However, any pastor who has ever slipped out of a boring convention to chat with a colleague around the bookstand or who talks shop on the golf course understands the vital role that informal conversations play in shaping pastoral theology and practice. If the truth be known, pastors probably learn more from each other than from any other source. Refined by ongoing interaction with my pastor friends, ideas expressed here have been field-tested in the laboratory of life and distilled in the crucible of local churches of various sizes.

"Democracy," wrote Fosdick, "is based upon the conviction that there are extraordinary possibilities in ordinary people."[4] It seems to me that Christ builds His Church with that same conviction. I invite you to join me on a quest to realize your full professional potential by embracing Jesus' model of ministry and, in so doing, rekindle your romance for the pastorate.

ONE

The Maelstrom of Mediocrity

The Maelstrom, a tidewater whirlpool in the Lofoden Islands off Norway's northern coast, has been widely known for centuries for its strength and dangerous current. Since it poses a threat to ships, Edgar Allan Poe described it with great imagination in his celebrated short story titled *A Descent into the Maelstrom.*[1]

Poe's narrator is led to a high cliff on Helseggen mountain overlooking the Maelstrom by a man who survived a traumatic experience in this vicious vortex that swallows ships, animals, and anything else in its path. During a fishing trip, he and his two brothers encountered an awful storm that damaged their boat, washed the younger brother overboard, and pulled the survivors into the dreaded Maelstrom. The boat spun around and around, slowly descending for about an hour, with the man tightly grasping a ringbolt in the deck. The older brother at first stood at the back of the vessel holding on to a water cask so he would not be swept overboard, but he then suddenly moved toward the man and pried the ringbolt from his fingers. The older brother then used the ringbolt to secure himself. Aggravated by his brother's selfish action, the man took his place at the water cask.

As the descent into the abyss continued, the man noticed the movement of the current and various objects that were floating around them —a fir tree, wrecked ships, furniture, and barrels. He suddenly remembered that sometimes objects would wash ashore near Lofoden undamaged because they were in the current at exactly the right time and floated up to the surface when the whirlpool calmed down. He observed that the cylinder-shaped objects descended slower than the rest. With this knowledge, he tied himself to the water cask that his brother had left behind, tried unsuccessfully to get his brother to do the same, cut himself free from the sinking boat, and jumped into the raging waters. The plan worked, as his barrel's shape slowed its descent. He helplessly watched as his brother and their boat descended to a watery grave at the Maelstrom's bottom.

Eventually, the man and his barrel began to rise from the depths during the whirlpool's calming period. He surfaced and was rescued by fellow mariners who acknowledged that his hair had changed from black to white but refused to believe his tale. The man does not expect the narrator to believe it either, for he ends the story with these words: "I can scarcely expect you to put more faith in it than did the merry fishermen of Lofoden."

Christian ministry, by its very nature, is *countercultural,* and yet the dominant culture shapes our work more than we would like to admit.

Nowhere is this more evident than in our growing acceptance of under-achievement. Slowly but surely, we are being swept along in the mael-strom of mediocrity—a strong and dangerous current that keeps us from rising up to maximize our God-given potential.

You do not need a special gift of discernment to see what is happening throughout the land. When the late TV anchorwoman Jessica Savitch received an honorary degree from Columbia College back in 1983, her challenge to the students included the following assessment of the way things were at that time:

> As a reporter, I have had a chance to observe people at the top of just about every field. And it makes no difference if they are male or female, black or white, old or young, the people I observed succeeding are those who have been taught or who teach themselves to strive for excellence. The pleasure comes from knowing you have done a job the best way you know how. It seems to me, however, in our modern society that there is very little done these days in pursuit of excellence. But whatever there is, it stands out for its rarity.[2]

If excellence was rare in 1983, it is even rarer now. Mediocrity is mainstream. Its waters transcend all human categories—race, nationality, gender, occupation, socioeconomic class, and so on. According to data collected by the Gallup Organization, less than 30 percent of American workers are *fully engaged* at work; 55 percent are *not engaged*; 19 percent are *actively disengaged,* meaning that they are not only unhappy at work but also regularly share those feelings with colleagues. Furthermore, the longer employees stay with the same job, the less engaged they become.[3] My hunch is that you have at least one of the actively disengaged in your church, easily identified during worship services by folded arms and a facial expression that says, "Preacher, bless me if you can!"

Those who try to excel in the workplace are certainly going against the flow, and their behavior is disdainfully labeled schmoozing or kissing up to the boss because it shows up the average worker. Americans do not want mediocre performance in surgery, but we seem to accept it in almost every other field.

This cultural phenomenon should not surprise anyone, considering the well-documented lowering of academic standards in our nation's schools. Unsuspecting kids step into the shallow, subtle currents of educational mediocrity with little or no thought of where the waters may lead them. Alarming test scores reveal that most U.S. children are underachieving, because at all ability levels they lag behind children in many European and East Asian nations. Perhaps even more disturbing is that our own expectations have slipped far below what they used to be.

Outside the classroom, our youth are inundated with the "slacking is cool" message from pop music, television, movies, and ads. Teens who take responsibility are labeled geeks, nerds, and other less-flattering terms; they soon become the objects of ridicule and harassment. Eager to gain acceptance from the in crowd, many gifted young folk settle for less than their best. The waters are rising and swirling.

"A descent into the maelstrom" could continue in college, as academic-performance lessons learned in elementary and secondary schools are often reinforced there. Most major universities now award a significantly diluted bachelor's degree. Can you believe that many university English majors are no longer required to read Shakespeare or Chaucer! Grade inflation at our colleges and universities gives new meaning to the term "higher education."[4]

It's no surprise that underachieving students usually become underachievers in the workforce. We know them well; they are our church members, friends, relatives, and neighbors. Many of these would-be climbers showed great promise in the formative years but somehow got caught in the cultural undercurrent and settled for professional mediocrity. They can be identified by one or more of the following tendencies:

- Inconsistent or insufficient effort
- A lack of real engagement
- Ambivalence in decision making
- Lack of follow-through
- Disorganization
- Inability to reach goals
- A tendency to quit things just as one begins to achieve success
- Procrastination
- Involvement in jobs and situations that demand less than one's capabilities

- A paralyzing fear of failure

We have no problem identifying underachievement in others. As you perused the list of tendencies, names of colleagues, friends, and family members probably came to mind. Perhaps you were saddened by thoughts of what might have been. But what about you? Did you see yourself there? To recognize these potential-inhibiting patterns in your own life is to take the initial steps of the joyful journey into a more fruitful ministry. Remember, you do not have to be sick to get better.

It is much easier to recognize underachievement than to understand its underlying causes. In *Your Own Worst Enemy* (the first book devoted exclusively to adult underachievement), Dr. Kenneth Christian sheds light on this subject by describing 12 "self-limiting styles,"[5] presented here in summary form:

- **Sleepers:** A style seen most often in those from families or communities without models or traditions of high achievement. Sleepers lack accurate information about themselves, the extent of their talent, and ways to express it. A lack of support, opportunities, and guidance often play a role in the failure of sleepers to make early contact with their possibilities, as does a parental preference not to spoil or inflate them.

- **Floaters/coasters:** Aware of their abilities, they see opportunities, and often are even pursued by others, but rarely act on their possibilities. Some are temperamentally hesitant and slow to participate; others can be emotionally withdrawn or indolent and lacking in ambition. Their chief characteristics are passivity, lack of initiative, and disengagement.

- **Checkmates:** Have multiple but contradictory ambitions and feel hopelessly immobilized. Checkmates are often perfectionists who unconsciously fear change and arrange their lives so as to make change virtually impossible.

- **Extreme non-risk-takers:** Focus totally on minimizing risks in their lives; avoid situations in which they could possibly fail; gravitate toward occupations, relationships, and activities that do not present serious challenges or reflect their real interests.

- **Delayers:** Make postponing major decisions and commitments their central theme; procrastinate; miss deadlines; postpone the onset of adult life, and drift, evading permanence, engagement, and seriousness; sample many things superficially.

- **Stop-shorts:** Aware of their abilities, stop-shorts entertain ambitions and make significant progress but firmly hold back from reaching their goals. Their arrested progress is often related to a fear of completing a life step or of taking on some role that will be the outcome of fully realizing an aim. They take course requirements but do not complete the thesis, get a certificate but do not embark on the related career, finish law school but never pass the bar, suffer writer's block and fail to complete the novel.

- **Self-doubters/self-attackers:** Block their success by holding high standards they feel they can never possibly meet and for which they seldom strive; emphasize their own faults and failings; often feel that any personal accomplishment was a fluke. They avoid demands and expectations out of a fear of failing.

- **Charmers:** Have good intentions but are inclined to use their engaging interpersonal abilities as a substitute for effort; often use a disarming sense of humor to diffuse criticism when they let things slide; develop a pattern of unreliability.

- **Extreme risk-takers:** Energetic and impulsive, they limit their success by habitually taking unnecessary risks; would rather fail in a blaze of glory than succeed through patient effort.

- **Rebels:** Aggressively strike out at the world and resist authority; unwilling to conform; suspicious of what they feel are others' attempts to exploit or control them.

- **Misunderstood geniuses:** Build a life around the notion that their talent sets them apart from others and that their lack of success is due to the misunderstanding, jealousy, and incompetence of others; use excuses; say their ideas are not mainstream or are too advanced for others to understand them; are temperamental.

- **Best-or-nothings:** Highly talented people for whom success comes easily or not at all; will not participate, if they cannot be the very best at something; progressively drop one activity after another; narrow their lives down to a few activities at which they clearly excel.

Your Own Worst Enemy is a must read for those who are serious about breaking the habit of adult underachievement. Filled with persuasive case studies, it offers scholarly yet practical advice for breaking through the barriers that keep us from approaching our potential. A radio interview featuring Dr. Kenneth Christian became the catalyst for this book, and since there are so few people writing on the subject of adult underachievement, I have drawn extensively from his groundbreaking research. Yet my primary focus has remained on the somewhat unique factors related to underachievement in the pastoral ranks—the subject of the next chapter.

I would be remiss to omit attention deficit disorder (ADD) and attention deficit hyperactivity disorder (ADHD) from any discussion of underachievement, since the term consistently appears on the lists of symptoms for both of these conditions. Unfortunately, many of those who have been diagnosed with adult ADD or ADHD were labeled as lazy, slow-learning, underachieving, problem kids—a heavy burden to bear when you already know that you have disappointed yourself and others. Prescription medications and professional counseling may assist these folk in focusing on the task at hand, increasing their productivity, enhancing their relationships, and relieving the load of false guilt.

Now before looking further at underachievement, I want to say a brief word about its opposite—*overachievement*. Predictably, this term has been popularized amid the maelstrom of mediocrity. You often hear it in connection with men like Jim Leonhard and Buddy Marston. But what does the word actually suggest? Can a person really achieve more than he or she is capable of? Of course not. *Overachiever* is a misnomer; yet, we have applied it to people who achieve more than they *should*— that is, more than others expect of them. I theorize that the average Joes and Janes of the world are quick to label the maximizing person an overachiever because it implies an impossible level of performance, thus excusing the mediocrity in their own lives.

TWO

Good Is Not Good Enough

Most ministers are *good* ministers who plan *good* worship services, preach *good* sermons, render *good* pastoral care, run *good* board meetings, implement *good* programs, and offer *good* counseling. Therein lies a problem because, in the words of Jim Collins, "good is the enemy of great" and we must transcend "the curse of competence" in order to be all that we can be in the Lord's army.[1] Good may be good enough for the average person living in a world where mediocrity is not only tolerated but often celebrated. However, good is not good enough for the God-called pastor when better is possible. While it's true that no one ever realizes his or her *full* potential, each of us should be striving to close the actualization gap between where we are and where we could be.

As we have already seen, one factor that contributes to under-achievement is our society's pervasive accommodation to it. There are many more. In this chapter, we will focus on those factors that are somewhat unique to the pastoral ministry; some deserve more ink than others.

UNDEFINED PURPOSE

Some individuals seem to have a very clear understanding of their life's purpose, like the young college student wearing a T-shirt emblazoned with the simple statement "I am going to be a doctor." The sign on the back of his bicycle reads, "I am going to be a Mercedes!" The legendary Sam Walton was driven by this mission statement: "So long as I live, I will continue to reduce prices."

Most people are not quite that sure about the direction of their life, even some of us preachers. Like the *Flying Dutchman,* some appear to be condemned to perpetual wandering. Too many lives are characterized by trivial pursuits with lots of things to do, places to go, and people to see but no real sense of purpose.

Jesus announced His life's mission in a dramatic scene at His hometown synagogue. Unrolling the scroll of Isaiah, He read these words: "The Spirit of the Lord is on me, because he has anointed me to preach good news to the poor. He has sent me to proclaim freedom for the prisoners and recovery of sight for the blind, to release the oppressed, to proclaim the year of the Lord's favor" (Luke 4:18-19). When all eyes were upon Jesus, He declared, "Today this scripture is fulfilled in your hearing" (v. 21). In a somewhat self-fulfilling statement, Jesus went on to say, "No prophet is accepted in his hometown" (v. 24). How did the hometown congregation respond? They were meaner than the Philadelphia crowd who booed Santa Claus. The narrative informs us that their anger prompted them to drive Jesus out of town to the brow of the hill with intentions to toss Him down the cliff. With friends like that, who needs enemies! Jesus, confident in His life purpose, "walked right through the crowd and went on his way"(v. 30). On another occasion, in His dramatic encounter with Zacchaeus, Jesus succinctly stated His purpose: "The Son of Man came to seek and to save what was lost" (19:10).

Jesus' life had an overarching purpose, and the Gospel narratives verify that He was true to it, even though His closest followers attempted to dissuade Him at times. He knew the Father's will and resolutely acted on it. Obedience so characterized Jesus' life that near the end, in the so-called high-priestly prayer, He could bow before His Father and declare, "I have brought you glory on earth by completing the work you gave me to do" (John 17:4).

Yes, Jesus lived with a clear sense of mission and purpose; to be truly *Christian* (i.e., Christlike) ministers, we must do the same. When asked to describe their calling into professional ministry, 137 of the 149 maximizing pastors taking my survey indicated that they have a very clear and strong sense of calling; another 10 respondents described their calling as fairly clear and strong. A strong sense of divine calling is foundational to ministry effectiveness. But how do we ascertain God's purpose for our life? The following vignette offers some valuable insight.

Just as the Great Revolution was getting underway in Russia, a rabbi on his way to the synagogue was stopped at gunpoint by a soldier. With his rifle pointed directly at the rabbi, the soldier said in a gruff voice, "Who are you, and what are you doing here?" The rabbi replied with a question of his own: "How much do they pay you for doing this job?" The soldier replied, "Twenty kopecks." Then the rabbi said, "I will pay you twenty-five kopecks if every day you stop me right here and ask me those two questions."[2]

"Who are you? What are you doing here?" Two fundamental questions that go together like peanut butter and jelly. If and how we answer them determines whether or not we have a clearly defined purpose in life. We have all wrestled with these queries and testified to our calling before credentialing boards. The majority of us have studied and/or taught Warren's *Purpose-Driven Life*. And yet, some are still suffering a mild case of vocational amnesia.

In an article titled "Misdirected Calls," William Easum admits that his own journey into pastoral ministry was somewhat misdirected. He testifies that the call to a more apostolic role was prostituted by those who advised him to be the pastor of a church. According to Eph. 4:12, the role of pastors is "to equip the saints for the work of ministry" (NRSV); yet, so many who hold the pastoral position see themselves as chaplains or counselors, not equippers. While it's true that Jesus said, "Feed my sheep" (John 21:17), Easum reminds us that the ancient shepherd got the sheep into a pasture where they could graze, grow, and produce wool. The primary goal was not the care and feeding of the sheep but what the sheep would produce.[3]

Since shepherd is our dominant pastoral image and we have attached warm-and-fuzzy notions to that role, it will be difficult—if not impossible—for some of us to embrace the call to equip the saints. After all, we get lots of affirmation when we simply take care of their needs. Could it be that many have been duped into following the wrong call? Is it unkind for Easum or me to suggest that those who haven't sensed a strong, specific call to be a pastor should take action and find their rightful place somewhere else in God's world? Release from a misguided calling can be liberating if it leads to a true one.

At the risk of sounding judgmental, I am coming to believe that we are sanctioning far too many men and women who enter this work for the wrong reasons—to please family members, to be in a position of authority, or to simply help people. Now let's be honest—most of us have struggled, to some degree, with these secondary motives. There's nothing inherently wrong with longings to please your family, to lead, or to help people, but these desires should never become the main motivation for becoming a pastor. The pastoral calling has its genesis in the will of God. Thus He provides the grace to keep us going when the going gets tough, and the gifts to make our work effective. It is axiomatic—God never calls us to do anything but what He enables us to do.

In addition to this deep sense of calling to be a pastor, maximizing pastors generally speak of specificity in their calling to serve a particular people in a particular place for a particular season. God calls and so does the church. The divine call, realized in a thunderclap experience or a gradual dawning, must be tested and confirmed by an ecclesiastical call. The call of God and the call of the church are not synonymous, but life is certainly good when the two come together.

Our identity should be based upon who we are as God's children, not upon what we do. Jesus and the New Testament writers would have us to remember all that we are:

- Chosen people
- Gifted members of Christ's Body
- Fruit-bearing branches
- Witnesses
- Living sacrifices
- More than conquerors
- Christ's ambassadors
- Aliens and strangers in the world
- Citizens of heaven
- The reflection of God's glory
- The Bride of Christ
- The aroma of Christ among those who are being saved and those who are perishing
- Royal priests
- Ministers of reconciliation
- The light of the world
- The salt of the earth
- Fishers of men
- Servants
- Slaves
- Soldiers

If you are struggling to maintain a positive self-image, you can go to the airport and page yourself or simply ponder the implications of these biblical images. Anchored here, we can survive the storms of life that may even remove us from a ministry assignment.

Even so, we pastors find it virtually impossible to distinguish between our identity and our vocation. We readily identify with the story of Yehudi Menuhin, the renowned maestro and violinist who held worldwide audiences spellbound with his conducting and virtuoso playing. He made his performing debut in San Francisco at the age of 7 and launched his global career at the age of 12 with a concert at Carnegie Hall. In his memoirs, *Unfinished Journey,* Menuhin tells how his love affair with the violin began. From the time he was only 3 years old, his parents took him to concerts in New York where he heard the first violinist Louis Persinger. Little Yehudi was enchanted by Persinger's solo passages.

"During one such performance," Menuhin wrote, "I asked my parents if I might have a violin for my fourth birthday and Louis Persinger to teach me to play it." A family friend gave him a toy violin, made of metal with metal strings. He was furious and threw it to the ground, despite the fact that he was too small to handle a full-sized violin. Reflecting on that scene, Menuhin said that he wanted nothing less than the real thing because "I did know instinctively that to play was to be."[4]

The God-called pastor knows that serving the Lord in this role is "to be" and probably doesn't need the reminder that we are most fulfilled and fruitful when we are expressing the deepest gifts that are truly who we are. As the Nazis were moving into the Netherlands, Henry Kramer, a Dutch theologian, was asked by a group of Christian laymen, "Our Jewish neighbors are disappearing from their homes . . . what must we do?" Kramer replied, "I cannot tell you what to do. I can tell you who you are. If you know who you are, you will know what to do." These persons became part of the Dutch Resistance Movement.[5]

"If you know who you are, you will know what to do." I have a hunch that this simple statement resonates with you. Ponder the real-world ramifications of this truth. Perhaps, we can get our minds around them better by expanding Kramer's comment to read: "If you know who you are, you will know what to do *and how to do it.*"

When the noted English architect Sir Christopher Wren was directing the building of a famous cathedral, some of the workers were interviewed by a passing journalist. He asked the three workers the same question, "What are you doing?" The first said, "I'm cutting stone for ten shillings a day." The second replied, "I'm putting in ten hours of my life every day on this job." The third answered, "I'm personally helping Sir Christopher Wren to construct one of London's greatest cathedrals."[6] Which one of the three men do you suppose rendered the best work?

What are you doing? Are you serving the church or the God who called you? "Cutting stone" or personally cooperating with the Christ who promised to build His Church? Your honest answers to those questions will determine how you approach ministry. Some photographs from an

Italian newspaper over a century ago showed mounted cavalry going through some daring maneuvers with their horses. Underneath the pictures was this caption: "They're doing their best, for the king is present."

BAGGAGE FROM ONE'S PAST

I have never owned a paperback romance novel and probably never will. However, one being read by a fellow passenger on Washington's Metro train did pique my interest because of its intriguing title—*Woman Without a Past.* It caused me to wonder about its plot. Was it the story of someone suffering with amnesia? Perhaps she just appeared on the scene, unwilling to discuss her life history. Or maybe she was an undercover spy working for the CIA. I will never know. However, I do know that every person really does have a past—the good, the bad, and the ugly—which has the potential to color everything we do today.

You will recall that most underachieving sleepers grew up in families and/or communities devoid of affirmation. For them, home was a place where seldom was heard an encouraging word. What's worse is that the sleeper probably heard more than his or her fair share of discouraging words—negative feedback that goes a long way in shaping a person's self-identity. It would be impossible to overstate the damage caused by careless adults who imply or actually say to children, "You are dumb . . . lazy . . . ugly . . . clumsy." Some are tagged with an unflattering nickname, like my good friend "Monkey." Such terms are both descriptive and prescriptive. They tell you not only what people *think* of you but also what they *expect* from you. Before too long, a person can begin to see the description as a personal attribute that seems unchangeable, accept the role suggested by the put-down, and behave accordingly throughout his or her life. Perhaps you carry this burdensome baggage, having been on the receiving end of both verbal and nonverbal messages that have hampered your ability to fulfill God's destiny for your life. I would encourage you to revisit your formative years; ponder the life-limiting messages you have accepted at face value; forgive those who failed to cultivate your potential; avoid the blame game; surround yourself with affirming friends; and, most importantly, bask in the unconditional love of God.

If you have been in vocational ministry for very long, you have been injured by someone under your care—"well-intentioned dragons" or those whose intentions were less than honorable. A pastor in Menomonie, Wisconsin, was brutally attacked by a church member who blamed the minister for the breakup with his wife. Marriage counseling had failed. According to published reports, the man tackled the pastor in the sanctuary, beat his head against a pew, hit him repeatedly with a wooden easel, bound his arms and legs with duct tape, forced him to drink whiskey through an animal syringe, and planned to stage a fatal automobile crash in hopes of discrediting the pastor's reputation in the community. After putting the pastor in his pickup truck, the assailant could not locate the minister's keys and returned to the sanctuary to search for them. Somehow the pastor managed to open the truck door and escape for help. In the aftermath of this incredible assault, the pastor was treated for broken ribs, cuts, bruises, and bite wounds. The former church board member served time for false imprisonment and recklessly causing bodily harm.

Most attacks on a pastor are not so direct and certainly not as bizarre. Those who oppose a pastor are more likely to demonstrate passive-resistant behavior or engage in a covert operation that involves forming alliances with the like-minded and planting questions that raise doubts about the pastor's competence and character—a subversive strategy that *indirectly* undermines the pastor's leadership. Direct and indirect attacks hurt; they injure our spirit; they rob us of joy; they sap our energy; they squelch spontaneity; they divert our attention from Kingdom work to just trying to survive. Thomas à Kempis reminds us of the value of adversity, even going so far to suggest that "it is good that we at times endure opposition and that we are evilly and untruly judged when our actions and intentions are good. Often such experiences promote humility and protect us from vainglory. For then we seek God's witness in the heart."[7] We understand that, we believe that, and we have even captured the essence of this thought in the popular saying, "What doesn't kill you makes you stronger!"—and yet this wonderful truth does little to ease the pain of personal attacks.

Isn't it ironic that those who are capable of bringing us the greatest joys in life—family and church members—are the very ones who can hurt us the most? That is true because our emotions are so deeply involved in those relationships that really matter to us. C. S. Lewis wrote of the vulnerability associated with love and offered a somber warning:

> To love at all is to be vulnerable. Love anything, and your heart will certainly be wrung and possibly be broken. If you want to make sure of keeping it intact, you must give your heart to no one, not even to an animal. Wrap it carefully round with hobbies and little luxuries; avoid all entanglements; lock it up safe in the casket or coffin of your selfishness. But in that casket—safe, dark, motionless, airless—it will change. It will not be broken; it will become unbreakable, impenetrable, irredeemable . . . The only place outside Heaven where you can be perfectly safe from all the dangers . . . of love is Hell.[8]

"A job without criticism is like a dog without fleas—hard to find and harder to keep."[9] Criticism—whether deserved or undeserved—comes with the pastoral assignment and prompts us to pray for the hide of a rhinoceros. An untamed tongue can be a weapon of mass destruction, and unkind words will penetrate even the thickest of skin.

How will you respond to criticism? The normal human reaction is to get angry, become defensive, and strike back in retaliation. Clearly, the Spirit-filled pastor would not and should not engage in a war of words with his or her critics. After all, Jesus said, "Love your enemies . . . pray for those who persecute you . . . turn the other [cheek]" (Matt. 5:44, 39, NRSV). I must confess, however, that there have been times in my pastoral journey when I felt like inscribing the names of a few difficult people on golf balls and driving them 300 yards!

Ventilation is another possible response to criticism. Wounded in spirit and seeking validation, some of us are more likely to tell our supporters about how we have been treated unfairly rather than bringing the matter to the One who really understands injustice. In so doing, we add fuel to the fire and polarize our people but fail to address the nagging issues.

And then there's capitulation, the "not-so-sweet surrender" to the critic's wishes. There are some battles that are worth fighting and some that are not. A wise pastor knows the difference. In an effort to keep peace, some of us crumble under criticism and yield to the desires of strong-willed lay leaders. "Change is stifled, growth stunted, and the direction of ministry is set by the course of least resistance, which as everyone knows, is the course that makes rivers crooked."[10] Pastors who surrender visionary leadership in the face of public challenges may keep the peace for a while but often harbor resentment against those church bosses who got their way.

Retaliation, ventilation, and capitulation have one thing in common—they all contribute to the emotional debris in a pastor's life. Pastors lead best when they lead from the heart; however you cannot lead effectively when the heart is cluttered with unresolved issues from the past.

In light of our identification with Jesus and His ongoing mission, we should expect hurts even if we cannot fully embrace them. Even winners get wounded in the battle. Having been the target of some friendly fire on more than one occasion, I am convinced that it is much more difficult to recover from emotional wounds than physical injuries. Here's what happens more often than we would like to admit: We hold on to hurts long after the intensity of our pain has abated. They are nursed and rehearsed. As we replay old tapes of caustic comments or reread critical letters, our blood pressure rises. We finally file the offense away in the archives of our mind and piously proclaim that we have forgiven and forgotten it. Most of us guard our past as we would our weight, revealing it cautiously to those we trust but inadvertently to everyone. Then, at the most inopportune time, the unresolved hurt raises its ugly head and gets projected into one of our current relationships. Sadly, church members may be unfairly judged because they remind us of someone who mistreated us in the past. The memory of pain caused by the betrayal of a dear friend may keep us from entering into a prayer partnership that calls for authenticity and vulnerability. A pastor's frustration with a domineering mother may adversely affect how he or she deals with confident and capable female leaders in the local church.

"Anger is our sixth sense for sniffing out wrong in the neighborhood. What anger fails to do, though, is to tell us whether the wrong is outside or inside us. We usually begin by assuming that the wrong is outside us."[11] If, however, you are *overreacting* to minor offenses, the problem lies within and it probably stems from the hurts of your past. And some of us are subconsciously angry with God for placing us where He has. Like Jonah, we hate Nineveh and are worse in our obedience than in our disobedience.

The tendency is to deny or justify unresolved anger toward God and others because there seems to be little room for it within our theological constructs. I would argue that to be truly Christian is to be authentically confessional. So let us acknowledge the baggage of our painful past, release it to God, and experience healing for our damaged emotions. The sooner, the better.

Several key life lessons emerge from John's account of Lazarus's resurrection. The narrative clearly teaches us about the dual nature of Jesus, the God-man. Jesus' humanity caused Him to weep with those He loved; Jesus' divinity enabled Him to resurrect a dead man. Less obvious is the truth that those who have been raised to new life in Christ still struggle with binding graveclothes and often need someone else's assistance to really get free. Counselors, both professional and nonprofessional, are among Jesus' helpers. I find it interesting that we live and serve among people who are comfortable with counseling as a means of inner healing and yet most of us "wounded healers" (Henri Nouwen's term)[12] avoid it like the plague. Are we physicians of the soul who can heal ourselves? I don't think so. Could it be that we fear the transparency and vulnerability required by the counseling process? Likely.

Do not hold on to the past. Alan Alda metaphorically expressed this idea in the offbeat title of his autobiography *Never Have Your Dog Stuffed*. From the childhood moment when his dog is returned from the taxidermist's shop with a hideous expression on his face and he learns that death cannot be undone, through his lengthy effort to find compassion for his mentally ill mother, Alda learned that true happiness means letting go and embracing change.[13] "The past is a dead issue and we can't gain any momentum moving toward tomorrow if we are dragging the past behind us."[14] A maximizing pastor surrenders a painful past for a fruitful future.

ILLEGITIMATE EXPECTATIONS

Pastoral ministry emerges from the call of God; however, the church must also call for there to be authentic leadership in the name of Christ. William Willimon rightfully refers to the clergy as "community persons" with a bivocal calling.[15] If you ever start feeling rather smug about *the call* being your personal possession, remember this—you have a ministry *only* because of the church's need for leaders, and there is a sense in which we get some direction from the people we serve. The central liturgical gesture of ordination, the laying on of hands, symbolizes the church's validation of God's calling upon your life.

Given the communal nature of the pastoral vocation, we should not be surprised that church members frequently possess strong opinions about how the pastor should invest time and energy. Ministerial duties consisted of little more than preaching and visitation in the good old days. It may shock younger readers to discover that those were the basic expectations during my first pastorate in the mid 1970s. Church members wanted me to deliver two sermons a week, lead the Wednesday night prayer meeting, and visit in the hospitals and in their homes at least twice annually.

Well, times have changed dramatically and so have the expectations of the laity. Some demands are valid, inasmuch as they are rooted in biblical teaching and historical practice within the church. Everyone agrees that a pastor should teach, preach, pray, administer sacraments, equip God's people for service, marry and bury people. Scriptures and tradition confirm these pastoral functions. However, I have come to believe that corporate America has done more than either Scripture or tradition to define the pastoral office in recent years. Nowadays, lay leaders have cast pastors in the CEO role and, strangely enough, most of us have readily embraced it with little or no thought about how such an identity may detract from the core work of our pastoral vocation.

Pastors wear so many hats but some fit better than others. William Willimon calls on seminaries to train ministers in the "arts of peculiarly *pastoral* administration" and cautions:

> The pastor as manager can be an all too appealing image for pastors who lack the creativity and the courage to do more than simply

maintain the status quo of the church—to keep the machinery oiled and functioning rather than pushing the church to ask larger, more difficult questions about its purpose and faithfulness. Pastors are called to lead, not simply to manage. Many of us serve churches that have become dysfunctional, unfaithful, and boring. Having lost a clear sense of our mission, we diffuse ourselves in inconsequential busyness. Lacking a sense of the essential, we do the merely important. Any pastor who feels no discontent with the church's unfaithfulness, who is too content with inherited forms of the church, is not just being a bad manager, but has made the theological mistake of surrendering the joyful adventure of pastoral ministry for the theologically dubious office of ecclesiastical bureaucrat.[16]

While some illegitimate expectations of the pastor have been largely shaped by secular images of the successful executive, others arise from the selfish, misguided desires of church members who want to be served rather than serve. Newsflash: there are a few folk under your care who are totally convinced that God called you to be their unpaid life coach or personal porter, on call 24/7/365. The Barna Group research reveals that churchgoers expect their pastor to juggle an average of 16 major tasks.[17] Afflicted with the "disease to please,"[18] many have forsaken the historical pastoral care model that utilized mostly corporate, priestly functions in favor of care that is highly individualized and heavily influenced by therapy techniques. The result is a preoccupation with the holy huddle.

To make matters worse, every congregation seems to have two-legged *bird dogs*—those who enjoy sniffing out situations that need the pastor's attention and pointing him or her in that direction. They specialize in dumping guilt on us with comments like: "Pastor, how long has it been since you visited Sister Smith in the nursing home?" "Pastor, you've got to start something for our young adult singles . . . we're losing them as soon as they graduate high school." Or "Pastor, the Lord has laid something on my heart . . . we need to start praying for revival at an early Monday morning prayer meeting like the one at First Church . . . you could share a brief devotional at 6 A.M. to prepare us for intercession." In response to that request, you may want to inform the bird dog that you are a "latter day saint!" Seriously, we all have learned that the best way to respond to bird dogs is to inform them that the Lord hasn't spoken to you about their concern and assure them that if He does, you will heed the call. You may go on to suggest that their burden may be a sign that the Lord wants them to take some initiative at that point.

I find it interesting and a bit bothersome that at the very outset of Jesus' ministry, Satan tried to define His work. You know the temptation story. During those 40 difficult days in the wilderness, the deceiver offers Jesus some attractive alternatives—stones to bread, political power, and miracles. He rejects them all because they did not square with the Father's purposes for His life. Pastor friend, there's an important life lesson here—ministry involves a crucial choice between doing God's work His way or our own. Are you clear about the pastor's proper work? If not, the enemy stands ready to steer you in the wrong direction. Temptation is an ongoing battle on this front. At times, pastors are asked why their ministry took a certain turn. Wouldn't it be refreshing to hear one of us honestly admit occasionally that "the devil made me do it!"

Unrealistic expectations may be partially explained by the paradoxical nature of the church. I believe it was Dr. Les Parrott who pointed out that the church is both divine and human, invisible and visible, local and universal, unified and diversified, holy and sinful, in this world and of the other world, invincible and vulnerable. I would add that the church is both an organism and an organization. Spirit-filled Christians often disagree over the pastor's role, given the fact that we tend to view the church in terms of either-or rather than both-and. For example, if your local church has bought into an organizational model of the church and the correlative CEO functions of the pastor, they will expect you to invest heavily in administrative tasks, developing programs and marketing the church. On the other hand, if the majority of your people see the church as an organism, they will press you to spend more time praying and less time promoting.

It seems to me that balance is the key. Given the paradoxical nature of the church (this-worldly and otherworldly), every church needs to address the leadership requirements that enable the congregation to address both realities. Church boards need to negotiate their official requirements (written understandings) in light of the pastor's gift mix, passion, aptitude, personality, and experience. At the end of the day, other qualified leaders—credentialed and noncredentialed—may need to assume some leadership responsibilities previously reserved for the senior pastor.

Unrealistic expectations drive pastors to distraction, if not to an early grave. If you've been at this for a while, you know that there are some people who stir up more dust than their pastor can sweep up. We become weary in well-doing, fatigued by faithfulness. The pastor's load is heavier than ever. "One reason many pastors become so exhausted by the demands of ministry is that they enter ministry with little basis for it other than 'meeting people's needs.' That is dangerous in a society of omnivorous desire, where people, not knowing which desires are worth fulfilling, merely grab at everything."[19] To avoid exhaustion, we must learn to kindly say no to unrealistic expectations and to stay grounded in a pastoral theology informed by biblical images.

It seems to me that people expect far more from us than God does. I am reminded of what Ed Vargo, National League supervisor of umpires, always said to new umpires, "You're expected to be perfect the day you start—and then improve!" Laypersons want us to preach with the effectiveness of Peter, practice intercessory prayer with the passion of Abraham, counsel with the wisdom of Solomon, coordinate volunteers with the leadership skills of Nehemiah, bring others to Christ with the zeal of Andrew, launch new congregations with the missionary spirit of Paul, build with the carpentry skills of Noah, coordinate worship music with the grace of David, and so much more. It can be tough living in the shadows of the bigger-than-life biblical characters, especially when laypersons forget that men of faith were not always faithful men. What's worse is to have one's ministry contrasted with the popular televangelists who can prepare their masterpiece messages without the distractions of the ongoing demands of a local church setting.

If multitasking were an Olympic sport, the gold medalists would likely be pastors. We spin lots of plates. Henri Nouwen insightfully notes that we seem to take "being busy and being important to mean the same thing."[20] It is both a bane and a blessing that modern technology has provided us infinite accessibility. Cell phones, computers, pagers, and so on, keep us constantly connected to our people, including those who want to be sure that we stay busy. Almost every call or e-mail adds to an already overwhelming to-do list. But we want to please people, and we make the mistake of trying to do everything church members expect of us, rather than focusing on the few things that would most please God.

Why do we do this? There is no simple explanation; it's a rather complex scenario that involves our almost insatiable desire to please people, to survive politically, and to have our ego needs satisfied. Let's face it. We derive a sense of significance from the work we accomplish, and it feels so good when people tell us how wonderful we are for doing it. "Pastor, I could never have made it without you" strikes a responsive chord in our hearts and we start believing it. Warning: adulation is addictive. Smitten with the affirmation of grateful people, we are apt to develop a messiah complex and seek out occasions where it can be reinforced. As we are meeting people's needs, they are meeting ours. Such codependency has devastating consequences.

Here's the bottom line: if we succumb to the temptation of trying to meet illegitimate role expectations, our ministry will become a mile wide and an inch deep. In the process, we may be robbing the laity of an opportunity for service and contributing to our premature demise.

DISORDERLY CONDUCT

Statutes defining disorderly conduct include a broad range of behaviors (fighting, threatening, making unreasonable noise, using obscene language, making obscene gestures, recklessly creating a risk, etc.) that cause *public* inconvenience. Few pastors are ever charged with it, especially since we stopped judging the quality of sermons by their volume! However, far too many of us are guilty of disorderly conduct that causes *personal* inconvenience, squanders time, and limits our effectiveness.

We often quote Paul's admonition about "redeeming the time" (Eph. 5:16, KJV) or "making the most of your time" (NASB), but its meaning may have somehow escaped us. We rush headlong from one appointment to the other, day in and day out, as if a modern paraphrase of the passage reads, "Hurry up!" Like the Energizer Bunny, we keep going and going and going. On the way, we observe people strolling along, standing around, or relaxing on outdoor patios and wonder aloud, "Don't these people have jobs?" Covetous of someone else's free time, we may miss their unspoken message analogous to the Eph. 5:16 passage—loosely translated "work smarter, not harder." I propose that we slow the hectic pace of our lives and embrace the notion that making the most of one's time does not mean working harder but working smarter through better life management.

Pastors *go* to work without *going* to work. The sheer nature and size of our assignment can be quite overwhelming. One pastor quipped, "I feel like a mosquito who just flew into a nudist colony; I know what to do but hardly know where to begin!" We can all identify with that feeling, can't we? In *White Collar Sweatshop,* journalist Jill Andresky Fraser reports that over 25 million Americans now work more than 49 hours per week and at least 8.5 percent of the workforce chalks up at least 60 hours per week.[21] I believe it's safe to say that the majority of pastors who are not bivocational log more than 50 hours per week in ministerial functions. God's grace somehow enables us to grin and bear it when tormenting church members insist that we only work one day a week. It is not uncommon for bivocational pastors, the unheralded heroes of the church, to burn the candle at both ends and hold two full-time jobs.

Given the breadth and depth of pastoral ministry, careful stewardship of our time must become a top priority. It seems to be more valuable than ever before. "We used to *pass the time,* as though it was something free that we were only too happy to share with others; now we *spend time* as though it's some kind of commodity to be bought and sold."[22] Time management experts encourage us to log all our activities for a few weeks so that we can see where we are spending our time and make adjustments accordingly. Try it. You will likely be surprised by the amount of time spent on the "soft addictions"—seemingly harmless habits that make even busy lives feel empty.[23] The list includes but certainly is not limited to the following activities: watching too much television, surfing the Internet, playing video games, checking investments, shopping, daydreaming about a better ministry assignment, and so on. Our ability to find more time for life-enriching endeavors hinges on our willingness to call these addictions by their rightful name and to seek God's help in finding freedom from their dominion over us.

Since so much of our work is done out of the public eye, we are particularly susceptible to time-thieves. A pastor could easily spend two hours per day handling e-mail chores. I recommend that you deal with these only once or twice a day, minimizing the distractions and allowing you to focus on ministry priorities. Most of us have had our fill of spam (unsolicited commercial messages) and meat loaf (forwarded messages, jokes, and other noncommercial e-mail messages sent to a large number of people). It takes so much of our valuable time to download these unwanted e-mails, review them, and send them to the trash bin. Besides, computers themselves seem to demand so much attention—especially when they get infected with a virus. If you suffer from techno-angst, resist the temptation to toss the baby (computer) out with the bath water. My advice is to make friends with a Christian computer geek who not only will help you discover the ministry benefits of the latest technological devices but also can exorcize their "demons" when necessary!

Full-time pastors are *flexecutives,* professionals whose hours and place of work are flexible. We do not punch a time clock, but like the family practitioner of a bygone era, we are always on call. If we pastors do not prayerfully and intentionally order our lives, someone else will do it for us. And that's OK—sometimes. In fact, the communal nature of our calling requires us to respond in a timely manner to the legitimate needs of those we serve. Jesus did. You will recall that on the way to resurrect the ruler's daughter, Jesus stopped to heal the bleeding woman who clutched His cloak and demanded His immediate attention. His miraculous feeding of the 5,000 was certainly not a prescheduled dinner on the grounds. Two blind men received their sight because Jesus stopped His journey from Jericho long enough to touch their eyes. These three unplanned interruptions and many more became the occasions for Jesus to demonstrate His limitless grace and power. We should be as open to such delightful diversions, because our best pastoral work seldom appears on the to-do list. I prefer to call them divine appointments, because it is God who orchestrates those collisions between extremely busy pastors and extremely needy people.

In the children's story, Winnie-the-Pooh and Piglet take a quiet evening walk together. Finally Piglet breaks the silence and asks, "When you wake up in the morning, Pooh, what's the first thing you say to yourself?" "What's for breakfast?" answers Pooh. "And what do you say, Piglet?" "I say, I wonder what exciting thing is going to happen today!"[24] Exciting things happen almost every day of a pastor's life. If, however, we wait for an emergency phone call or an e-mail request before setting the course of our daily functions, we may allow the urgent matters to crowd out the most important ones.

Let me be clear at this point. Few pastors waste a lot of time in trivial pursuits, unless you put managing the church in that category. It could be argued that someone has to keep the ecclesiastical machinery oiled; it is important work. In fact, almost everything we do is important. Thus, a serious effort to maximize our potential requires life management via a regular schedule that keeps us focused on the absolutely essential while allowing flexibility for those exciting things—those divine appointments.

What, then, are the absolutely essential functions of a maximizing pastor? It is my intention to offer a more comprehensive answer to that question in the proposed ministry model outlined in chapter 3. Suffice it to say at this point, my partial list would certainly include the tasks of preparing sermons, planning worship services, engaging the unchurched, making disciples, equipping leaders, praying, casting a vision, spending quality time with one's family, reading, and exercising. Your list may vary slightly. My hope, however, is that you will schedule your priorities, rather than just prioritize your schedule. If you do not live your life by priorities, chances are that you will be constantly haunted by false guilt—feeling as though you should always be doing something else, regardless of what you are doing.

These three questions should help you grapple with the issue of scheduling priorities with essential functions in mind: What are the basic role requirements of a pastor-leader? What functions provide the greatest return for the kingdom of God and the local church? What gives me the greatest sense of personal fulfillment? I can envision a productive church board meeting or weekend retreat with ministry-defining dialogue framed by these simple questions. Since most pastoral work occurs in relative obscurity, many church members are clueless about what we do between Sundays and are perplexed whenever we complain about not having enough time. These queries could open the channels of clear communication about your current responsibilities, enable you to set reasonable boundaries, empower laity to lighten your load, and free you to focus on those absolutely essential areas.

Years ago, I gave up the practice of making optimistic new year's resolutions in favor of crafting a weekly schedule driven by my life's mission and objectives. Adapting Dr. Bill Burch's model, I prayerfully established goals to become a better person, a better partner, a better parent, and a better professional (see Appendix 1). The behaviors that would enable me to reach those goals became a part of my weekly regimen (see Appendix 2). For instance, the goal to lower my cholesterol count called for cardiovascular workouts on my treadmill at least five days per week. So I inserted those sessions into my calendar, along with the other absolutely essential activities that resulted in personal and professional growth. The genius of the plan is its simplicity. Experience has taught us the value of setting aside blocks of time for sermon preparation and maintaining flexible regularity in the weekly routine. As you translate annual objectives into a weekly schedule, remember the wisdom of multitasking whenever one of those tasks is a no-brainer, and keep in mind that unfinished business is harder to complete the next time you come to it.

Life management seems to come naturally to pastors with a melancholic temperament. You know the type—the ones who put a premium on order and exactitude, like my friend who had all of his family's outfits color-coordinated, numbered, and neatly organized in their closets. I have this mental image of him waking his troops at the 0700 hour on Sundays and calmly but insistently declaring the family uniform colors for that day. If you possess a more spontaneous spirit, the intentional ordering of your life will be more of a challenge, but it's well worth the effort. Whether you adopt this scheduling plan or find another one that fits you better, life management must be a high priority for those intent on maximizing their potential.

It should be noted that charm and charisma often work against the discipline required for life management. Charmers have good intentions that seldom lead to consistent effort. If charming pastors can enjoy some measure of success by simply winging it, just think about what God could do through them if they practiced good old-fashioned discipline.

WANING SPIRITUAL PASSION

Many of us have been stirred by Dr. Bob Moorehead's "Fellowship of the Unashamed"—an inspirational essay often mistakenly attributed to an African martyr. The truth is that an African man had a copy of it on him when he was executed for his faith. It oozes with spiritual passion.

I am a part of the fellowship of the unashamed. I have Holy Spirit power. The die has been cast. I have stepped over the line. The decision has been made. I am a disciple of Jesus, and I won't look back, go back, hold back, let up, slow down, back away, hesitate, or be still! My past is redeemed. My present remade and my future re-aimed. I am finished and done with low living, sight walking, small planning, smooth knees, colorless dreams, tamed visions, mundane talking, chintzy giving, dwarfed goals, deficient faith, and cheap grace. I no longer need preeminence, prosperity, position, promotions, plaudits, prestige, or popularity. I don't have to be right, first, tops, recognized, praised, regarded, or rewarded. I now live by presence, lean by faith, love by patience, lift by prayer, and labor by power. My face is set, my gait is fast, my goal is heaven, my gift is grace, and my God is good. My road is narrow, my way is rough, my companions few, my guide reliable, my mission clear, and my power sufficient. I cannot be bought, compromised, detoured, lured away, turned back, diluted, distracted, deterred, or delayed. I will not flinch in the face of sacrifice, hesitate in the presence of the adversary, negotiate at the table of the enemy, ponder at the pool of popularity, wilt in the heat of the battle, or meander in the maze of mediocrity. I won't give up, shut up, let up, or burn up until I've preached up, prayed up, paid up, stored up, worked up, and stayed up for the cause of Christ. I am part of the fellowship of the unashamed. I walk in good company; I am a disciple of Jesus. I must go until He comes, give until I drop, preach until all know, stay until all go, and work until He stops. And when He comes to get His own, He'll have no trouble recognizing me. My colors will be clear![25]

His words probably strike a responsive chord in your heart, since most of us began the pastoral journey with similar fervor. We were zealous, fired up, ready to do battle with the enemy. Admittedly, some of us possessed more heat than light; nonetheless, there was no question about our allegiance to Christ and His cause. We identified with Wesley's challenge: "Give me one hundred preachers who fear nothing but sin, and desire nothing but God, and I care not a straw whether they be clergymen or laymen, such alone will shake the gates of Hell and set up the kingdom of heaven upon earth."[26]

That was then; this is now. Are you still ablaze with enthusiasm for the ministry? Has intensity given way to indifference? Has the flame flickered and nearly gone out with the passing of time? Warning: apathy tends to increase with age. Just as wisdom is often lacking in young pastors; zeal may be the missing ingredient in older ones. I have an idea that some of you, turned off by cheap emotionalism, have opted for a more stoical and cerebral approach to pastoral work. In so doing, you may be sending the wrong message to those under your watch. I suspect that our ministerial *motions* without *emotion* may give the impression that what we are about is not all that important. Pastors who are merely "trafficking in unfelt truth"[27] may be efficient but they are never effective. If you're going to be convincing, you've got to be convinced!

A while back, the flight attendants of a major airline engaged in a Withdrawal of Enthusiasm (WOE) campaign rather than launch an all-out strike. They tended to all their basic duties but did so without any enthusiasm, smiles, and warmth. As you might expect, it had a crippling effect on the company. The application is obvious. Robotic pastors who get the job done without enthusiasm may be considered faithful but are rarely fruitful.

There is no necessary conflict between intellectual honesty and emotional fervor. You need not discard a warm heart to acquire a keen mind, evidenced by both Jesus and the apostle Paul. We all know the shortest verse in the Bible—"Jesus wept" (John 11:35). What a simple, yet profound, statement. Our Lord wept publicly and, as far as we can discern, made no attempts to squelch His emotions. Paul, a man of great intellect, reminded the Ephesian elders that he had "served the Lord among them with great humility and *with tears*" (Acts 20:19, italics added). Emotional, passionate ministry is not what many would expect from the brilliant apostle/theologian. But this makes his tears all the more impressive.

Spiritual passion fuels every significant achievement in Kingdom work. If that's true, we need to be asking how a person can restore passion to his or her ministry? I offer three suggestions:

- Rekindle your love for Jesus. After all, discipleship in its purest and simplest form is all about an intimate relationship with Him. "'Come, follow me,' Jesus said, 'and I will make you fishers of men'" (Matt. 4:19). Think about it. The Lord of all creation wants to hang out with you and make you effective. Here's the problem: we seem to enjoy fishing more than following! Someone said, "The greatest threat to devotion to Christ is service for Christ." When the role becomes more important than the relationship, we surrender the joyful adventure of productive partnership for the futility of serving in the flesh.

    In a society steeped in the utilitarian view of man and defined by the Nike slogan "Just Do It," it is counterintuitive to abide with Jesus. We have heard Him say, "Apart from me you can do nothing" (John 15:5), and yet many of us act as if we really do not believe Him. Since the quality of every relationship hinges on regular communication, let us "Take time to be holy, / Speak oft with thy Lord; / Abide in Him always, / And feed on His Word" (William D. Longstaff).

If you began your professional journey with high-octane zeal but now seem to be running on empty, get back to the basics of Christianity 101—prayer, Bible reading, and worship—all means of grace for the weary soul. It is my hope that you will rediscover the pure delight of *being* with Him, even when there are a hundred things that you could be *doing* for Him. Perhaps we would do well to remember that Jesus commended Mary for sitting at His feet and listening (doing "what is better" [Luke 10:42]) while Martha prepared dinner. I will return to this subject later (chap. 3).

- Associate with people of passion. While the communal nature of the pastoral calling requires us to serve everyone, we can and should choose carefully those with whom we spend most of our time. John Maxwell notes that there are two types of people in the world: firelighters and firefighters. Firelighters believe in you, bring out the best in you, and stoke your soul's passion. Firefighters, on the other hand, are those negative thinkers who want to rain on everyone's parade.[28] You know the type. They carry a card in their wallet that reads, "In case of an accident, I'm not surprised!" Stay away from them, if you want to restore spiritual passion and maintain it. Sadly, there are many firefighters within the pastoral ranks—those who, for various reasons, have become critical and cynical. God could use you as an attitude adjuster; however, experience has taught me that my outlook goes south whenever I spend too much time with the whiners. I suggest that you establish a close connection to at least two or three firelighters, winners who are passionate about Christ and His cause. Their spirit is contagious.

In his book *Touch of Wonder,* Arthur Gordon recalls that years ago at the University of Wisconsin there was a club of some brilliant young men with some real literary talent. At each meeting, one of them would read a story or an essay he had written and submit it to the group's scrutiny. No punches were pulled; each work was mercilessly evaluated. The sessions were so brutal that the club members dubbed themselves "The Stranglers." The coeds formed a comparable group of their own known as "The Wranglers." Like their male counterparts, they read their manuscripts aloud; however, their criticism was much gentler. In fact, there was almost none at all. Instead, the Wranglers looked for kind things to say to each other. All literary efforts, however feeble, were encouraged. When an alumnus made an analysis of his classmates' careers, there were some interesting discoveries. Of all the bright young talent in the Stranglers, not one had made a literary reputation of any kind. On the other hand, a half dozen successful writers came from the ranks of the Wranglers—some of national prominence, including Marjorie Kinnan Rawlings who wrote *The Yearling.* Coincidence? I don't think so. Gordon notes that the basic talent in the two groups was about the same. The difference was that the Wranglers encouraged one another; the Stranglers discouraged each other and promoted self-doubt. "In choosing a name for themselves," wrote Gordon, "they had been wiser than they knew."[29]

- Remember what God has done for you. Remembrance is a golden thread woven throughout the fabric of Scripture. Because the children of Israel were prone to forget, God institutionalized memory of their deliverance from Egypt via the Passover festival. Jesus established the sacrament of the Lord's Supper as a reminder of how, by His sacrifical death and resurrection, we have been freed from sin's slavery. The best antidote for diminishing spiritual passion may be the occasional walk down memory lane, to recall just what the loving Liberator has done for us. Think back to the B.C. life you were living before God got a hold of your heart. Then ponder the radical change. We who were dead in transgressions have been resurrected to new life through Christ. His Spirit cleanses and empowers us. Our past is forgiven; our present is victorious; our future is secure. Besides, God has graced our lives with so many wonderful gifts—family, friends, healings, and so on. My dear dad would say, "If that doesn't light your fire, your wood is wet!"

MULTIPLE PERSONALITY SYNDROME

Knowing yourself and being yourself are critical to maximizing potential. Each of us is a one-of-kind original, an expression of God's creativity. There have been approximately 10 billion residents of earth since the beginning of time and not one of them is exactly like you. You are fearfully and wonderfully made, with your own personality, physical traits, gifts, interests, sense of humor, mannerisms, and so on. Now, nobody's perfect—in fact, Paul refers to us as "earthen vessels" (2 Cor. 4:7, KJV), which might be loosely translated "cracked pots." Yet the God who clearly recognizes our shortcomings recruited us "warts and all" for His ministry team. He saw something in us we did not see in ourselves. The old-timers were fond of saying, "God was more interested in our *availability* than our *ability.*" None of this should surprise us, considering God's choices for leadership in the past—a shepherd boy (David), one who lacked eloquence in speech (Moses), a shabby dresser (John the Baptist), a persecutor of the Church (Paul), and the original motley crew to whom Jesus entrusted His ongoing work—just to name a few.

I have a dim recollection of a Fox Sports broadcast that detailed the components of "the perfect NFL quarterback." With a bionic model proudly displayed, the experts focused on things like the strong arm of John Elway, the quick feet of Michael Vick, the torso toughness of Steve McNair, the field vision of Peyton Manning, the heart of Brett Favre, and so on. While the ideal quarterback may exist in the abstract, he doesn't play in the National Football League.

Likewise, an image of the ideal pastor exists in each of our minds. If I were constructing the perfect pastor, he would possess the vision of John Maxwell, the wisdom of Dennis Kinlaw, the face of Bill Hybels, the humor of Stan Toler, the optimism of Joel Osteen, the organizational genius of Rick Warren, the evangelistic spirit of Billy Graham, the "pipes" of Lloyd Ogilvie, and, of course, the courageous faith of the young African martyr. Given God's recruitment record, it's safe to say that there is no ideal pastoral persona. God uses ordinary people like you and me for this extraordinary assignment.

And yet, here's what tends to happen. Pastoral leaders, particularly the insecure and less experienced, often sell themselves short and start trying to be someone else. The ideal image can cause us to dwell on our deficiencies, to the point where we even question our call. Then our reasoning takes a twisted turn. We conclude that if indeed God has recruited us, He certainly cannot use us until we have experienced an extreme makeover. The "if only" game begins. "If only I could preach like . . ." "If only I could pray like . . ." "If only I could dress like . . ." And the "if only" list goes on and on. Sadly, many go to great lengths in emulating their heroes without ever developing their own unique ministerial identity.

I hesitate to employ the word *hypocrite* in my description of this phenomenon because it sounds so judgmental. Maybe *actor* is the more palatable term. You probably know, however, that the terms can be used synonymously, since the Greek word *hypocrites,* in ancient days, was used for an actor on the stage. Large amphitheaters seating 15,000 to 25,000 in the audience created some huge challenges for the soundmen of old. Without electronic amplification, actors wore large masks on their faces, containing hidden megaphones to project their voices. A hypocrite, then, is the one who wears a false face, who is an actor on a stage, and who appears to be someone he or she is not.

During my 10-year pastorate at Trevecca Community Church, I had the rare privilege of mentoring over 50 ministerial interns during their formative years of preparation. We talked and walked the pastoral life together for a full semester. Having heard several of their sermons, a perceptive church member remarked, "Most of these interns are trying to preach like Tim Green . . . they use his mannerisms, favorite phrases, and narrative style." I had to agree. But that's one of those "good news-bad news" scenarios. The good news is that Tim Green, Trevecca's chaplain, is a preacher par excellence—a masterful model for any and all of us. The bad news is that while emulating Tim, these students were not being themselves and his style did not fit everyone else as comfortably as it fits him.

The David and Goliath drama teaches us that everyone has to fight in his or her own armor. The shepherd boy refused Saul's tunic, coat of armor, helmet, and sword. Instead, he chose the staff, five small stones, the shepherd's bag, and the sling—all things that really fit him. If you read the Bible with some imagination, you have probably chuckled at the sight of the diminutive David clad in Saul's XXL outfit. I have a hunch that we look just as foolish whenever we try to don the armor of our pastoral heroes.

Speaking of chuckles, I once suffered through a solemn preacher's attempt at a stand-up comic routine prior to his sermon. His jokes, even if he had told them well, were not that funny. Punch lines were botched and his sense of timing was awful. It reminded me of a scene from the old *Gong Show,* but no one dared pull him off the platform. I learned later that a layperson had prompted him to insert more humor into his public ministry. Bad idea. Comedy simply did not fit his persona. On the other hand, I have a friend who is funnier than a barrel of monkeys outside the pulpit but when it's time to preach, he is as sober as a funeral director. Now something is wrong with that picture. Neither of these men were being themselves.

Samuel Johnson wrote, "About every man wastes part of his life in attempts to display qualities which he does not possess." Beware the multiple-personality syndrome. While it is advisable to adopt and adapt best practices from our professional colleagues, we can easily fall into the trap of squelching our uniqueness. Did you ever stop to think that your uniqueness may be the very thing necessary to reach certain types of people for Christ? Furthermore, have you considered that it takes a lot more energy to take on the character of someone else than it does to simply be yourself? Don't try to be someone else. Take off the mask —be yourself. Be that someone special God created you to be. Those who fight in their own armor will slay the giants.

THEOLOGICAL FOG SURROUNDING AMBITION

A friend recently sent me the following thought-provoking essay by an unknown author titled "The High Calling," which has been reprinted by The Frances Asbury Society. You may want to read it twice because it sets the stage for my point here.

If God has called you to be truly like Jesus, He will draw you into a life of crucifixion and humility, and put on you demands of obedience that sometimes will not allow you to follow other Christians.

47

In many ways He will seem to let other good people do things He will not let you do. Other Christians, and even ministers, who seem very religious and useful may push themselves, pull strings, and work schemes to carry out their plans, but you cannot do these things, and if you attempt them, you will meet with such failure and rebuke from the Lord as to make you sorely penitent.

Others can brag about themselves, about their work, about their success, about their writings, but the Holy Spirit will not allow you to do such things; and if you begin bragging, He will lead you into some deep mortification that will make you despise yourself and all your good works.

Others will be allowed to succeed in making great sums of money, or having a legacy left to them, or in having luxuries, but God may only supply you daily, because He wants you to have something far better than gold—a helpless dependence on Him—that He may have the privilege of providing your needs daily out of the unseen treasury.

The Lord may let others be honored and keep you hidden away in obscurity, because He wants to produce some choice, fragrant fruit for His coming glory, which can only be produced in the shade. God will let others be great, but keep you small. He will let others do a work for Him, and get the credit for it, but He will make you work and toil without others knowing how much you are doing. And then to make your work still more precious, He will let others get the credit for the work which you have done, and this will make your reward ten times greater when Jesus comes.

No doubt, reader responses to this clear warning against ambition will vary widely. Some of you may agree wholeheartedly, shout "Amen!" and proceed to post its message on your office wall. Others could cringe at the thought of "deep mortification, staying small and hidden away in obscurity"—wondering why such antiquated opinions should be included in a contemporary Christian leadership book. The latter group would identify with evangelist Jack Taylor's observation: "Our adversary would divide us by leading us to suppose that aspirations to succeed and humility were enemies; that the Holy Spirit deplores personal motivation; and that positive thinking is an enemy of total commitment."[30] Placed in juxtaposition, these two quotes reveal the diversity and evolution of thought on this subject.

Is there a place for ambition in the Spirit-filled life? If not, why not? If so, how does it take shape in our lives? Since the rise of the human potential movement in the 1960s, I believe Christian leaders—particularly in the Holiness tradition—have struggled to adequately answer these questions from a biblical perspective. Theological fog surrounding the subject of ambition, in some cases, has contributed to underachievement in the ministry.

Clearly, Christian leaders would not want to be perceived as cocky and arrogant. But sometimes we all can be overconfident. I remember one rookie pastor who dared to declare in his first report before a regional church assembly, "We are going to take Nashville!" The next year it was the same song, second verse. After three disappointing years, he humbly changed his tune.

I suppose we have all known a few megalomaniac pastors with delusional visions of grandeur—legends in their own minds. However, they are outnumbered 10 to 1 by those who feel poorly about themselves. Convinced that "fragrant fruit can only be produced in the shade," some sheepishly avoid any appearance of ambition and miss opportunities to extend their godly influence. They wonder how anyone could have the audacity to pray, as Jabez did, "Enlarge my territory" (1 Chron. 4:10). Those timid souls are content with current conditions and give the distinct impression that they lack motivation. I would hasten to add that some underachievers are not unmotivated but highly motivated to sabotage any chance of accomplishment—knowing that success carries with it the baggage called expectations.

Are ambition and humility mutually exclusive? I don't think so. Now, false humility involves denial of one's positive qualities, realizing that to acknowledge them is to be responsible for using them. The biggest cemetery is where unused talents are buried. Conversely, the truly humble person readily recognizes his or her abilities for what they are—gifts from God—and ambitiously invests them in the advancement of the Kingdom. Paul's testimony to the Corinthians reflects this spirit:

"By the grace of God I am what I am, and his grace to me was not without effect. No, I worked harder than all of them—yet not I, but the grace of God that was with me" (1 Cor. 15:10). Fearing that some believers may have considered his "confidence" as selfish ambition, Paul proceeds to give credit where credit is due: "Such confidence as this is ours through Christ before God. Not that we are competent in ourselves to claim anything for ourselves, but our competence comes from God. He has made us competent as ministers of a new covenant" (2 Cor. 3:4-6).

Understandably, most pastors are a bit reluctant to acknowledge their own competency, even when qualified by the Pauline phrase "from God." We are conflicted over ambition and must resolve this issue, if we are serious about maximizing our ministry potential. It may be helpful to distinguish between *selfish ambition* and *sanctified ambition*. "It's all about me" for those possessed by selfish ambition; sanctified ambition, on the other hand, is all about serving Jesus Christ and His cause.

Once again, the example of the apostle Paul is instructive. You will recall that Saul, before his life change and name change, was very ambitious. Acts 9 describes his actions: "Saul was still breathing out murderous threats against the Lord's disciples. He went to the high priest and asked him for letters to the synagogues in Damascus, so that if he found any there who belonged to the Way, whether men or women, he might take them as prisoners to Jerusalem" (vv. 1-2). His dramatic, blinding-light conversion experience did not transform him into a meek, passive person. Hardly. The New Testament record suggests that his ambition got converted with him. You get the feeling that if Paul were a dog, he'd bark louder than any other dog in the neighborhood; if he were a cat, he'd have the loudest "meow"; if he were a skunk, well—he'd be the biggest stinker in the woods! He was possessed with sanctified ambition.

In an e-mail devotional to the New Church Specialties partners, Executive Director Dr. Larry McKain focused on John 3:27, 30—a passage where John the Baptist responds to the Jews' prodding on the subject of human ambition. The forerunner replies, "A man can receive only what is given him from heaven. . . . He [Christ] must become greater; I must become less." McKain insightfully notes, "As spiritual leaders, we must regularly ask ourselves, 'Am I ambitious for myself or ambitious for Jesus Christ?' If my ambition is only for myself, my ministry will produce the unholy product of human pride. If my ambition is for Christ, it will produce excellence in ministry, maximize people's gifts, accomplish things seen as humanly impossible, and God will be praised! The ambition God sees as holy must be purified regularly by seeking His praise alone as the prime motivation of all we do."[31] Well said, my friend.

Sanctified ambition can be cultivated by positive self-talk, particularly that which is grounded in Scripture. Talking to oneself has sometimes been described as the first sign of insanity. Most psychologists, however, dismiss that notion and contend that talking to yourself may be good for you. Even so, I would caution against talking to yourself in public, since most people still consider it a bit odd.

Self-talk, whether positive or negative, has a way of becoming self-fulfilling prophecy. Gary McCord, the journeyman golf professional, likened himself to "just a range ball in a box of Titleists"[32] and his play confirmed this negative self-talk. He never won a tournament during his 23 years on the PGA Tour; instead, he suffered "negative bombardment on a daily basis" (his words, not mine). McCord's mediocre play and quick wit led him to the broadcaster's booth, a la Bob Uecker—the professional baseball player who parlayed mediocrity into popularity by mastering the art of self-deprecation.[33] Within the last few years, however, a new attitude has resurrected his playing career on the Champions Tour.

Some of you may identify with McCord's disappointing career and think of yourself as "just a range ball in a box of Titleists." Avoid the negative self-talk. Instead, fuel your sanctified ambition by the regular quotation of these biblical truths:

It is God who works in you to will and to act according to his good purpose (Phil. 2:13).

We proclaim him [Christ], admonishing and teaching everyone with all wisdom, so that we may present everyone perfect in Christ. To this end I labor, struggling with all his energy, which so powerfully works in me (Col. 1:28-29).

I can do everything through him who gives me strength (Phil. 4:13).

All things are possible with God (Mark 10:27).

Those with a passion to perform at a higher level stand awkwardly between the belief that they can do nothing and the belief that they can do anything. They are a study in duality: humble and ambitious. Let us be humble enough to acknowledge our utter dependence upon God; ambitious enough to partner with Him in a work that is humanly impossible.

DISCONTINUING EDUCATION

For some time now, licensing bodies in a number of fields have been imposing continuing education standards on those who hold professional credentials. The public derives some measure of comfort knowing that its lawyers, judges, doctors, teachers, counselors, real estate agents, and a host of other service providers periodically return to "school." But it is also a bit unsettling to discover that some do not. For example, I recently learned that Wisconsin dentists, unlike their colleagues in most other states, may continue their professional practice without mandatory continuing education. You might say it is like *pulling teeth* to get them back into the classroom! That bit of information will give me pause before the next crown or root canal. Here's why. Compulsory continuing education, usually measured by contact hours, sharpens the vocational skills of professionals and keeps them abreast of the latest and greatest developments in their field. Without it, all bets are off!

The church places a premium on the education of its clergy. A call to preach includes a call to prepare. Historically the preparation of would-be ministers usually occurred within the hallowed precincts of Bible colleges and seminaries. While most clergy still follow this educational path, a growing number choose directed studies through a variety of methods. Either way, the ministerial candidate usually is ordained once he or she has successfully completed the prescribed study requirements, met the ministry experience standards, passed the review of a credentialing board, and received an affirming vote by the constituency.

Ordination is considered a lifetime credential in most church circles, and so the minister need not appear before the credentialing board again. But in that lies a potential problem. Most ministers received training to do ministry in a world that no longer exists. If the ordained are never held accountable for continuing education in core competencies, they are likely to continue providing "modern" ministry in a postmodern world—oblivious to the underlying conditions that may render them ineffective or irrelevant. There are few things sadder than this.

Contemporary challenges heighten the seriousness of this issue. Within the past few decades there has been a slow but steady decline in the public's regard for organized religion. Apathy is giving way to antagonism, causing some to suggest that the 21st-century Church should engage our culture in the same way as our 1st-century counterparts engaged theirs. Whether you believe we are living in a post-Christian or pre-Christian era makes little difference. This truth remains—we must retool continually for missional effectiveness in a society where more and more people pursue spirituality outside of the institutional church. More than ever, we must assume the role of apologist for the faith and that will require us to carefully exegete both the Word and the world.

A changing culture calls for lifelong learning in every aspect of our work. Most of our how-to books, conference notes, and tapes procured during the last millennium are now obsolete. This new world demands new ways of doing ministry. However, it would be a costly miscalculation to focus on practics alone, to the neglect of biblical studies and theology. While it's true that the Bible never changes, the methods of understanding and communicating its life-giving message must be adapted to each generation. What's more, theology is dynamic and must be communicated in terms that are culturally relevant.

Continuing education has been institutionalized in most denominations, including my own. Legislation adopted in 1997 *encouraged* all Nazarene elders and deacons to continue a pattern of lifelong learning with a minimum of 20 contact hours each year. Four years later, they were *expected* to do so. Even so, only about 15 percent of our assigned ministers are actually earning the required two continuing educational units (CEUs). While pastors are asked to give an accounting of their progress in their annual report, little or nothing is actually done with the data.

There's amazing grace in our polity at this point, and I suspect the same could be said of most other "tribes." The Wesleyan Church, for example, describes continuing education as "a matter which is largely self-motivated and self-disciplined."[34] There are no mandated requirements in the Presbyterian Church of America; nor are there any in several congregationally governed denominations, including the Evangelical Free Church and Southern Baptists. The United Methodist Book of Discipline defines continuing education as at least one week per year and one month during one year of every quadrennium.[35] The Board of Ordained Ministry within each annual conference may add quantity definitions (i.e., contact hours) if it chooses. In the Free Methodist Church, there are no specific CEU requirements; however, each conference sets and monitors its own continuing education criteria.

Most of us serve within credentialing systems that allow the ongoing practice of ministry without required continuing education. Ecclesiastical grace at this point contributes to a climate of underachievement. What should be done? Is it time to revoke the credentials of those who flout the minimum requirements? Probably not. It would seem wise, however, for ecclesiastical leaders at every level to give more emphasis to continuing education both publicly and privately:

- Pastors could discuss the need for continuing education with their lay leaders, request that it become a line item in the annual budget, develop a long-term continuing education plan, and include a record of earned units in their résumés.
- Judicatory leaders can highlight the importance of ongoing training by modeling it, partnering with their pastors in the development of a continuing education plan, encouraging the laity to embrace it, and highlighting CEUs in their pastoral placement and review work with church boards.
- Educators can contribute to a lifelong learning ethos with ongoing

curriculum development and the use of various delivery systems (on-line classes, workshops, conferences, seminars, etc.).

Such simple steps would reinforce the positive behavior of those who are serious about professional growth. On the other hand, those who opt for arrested development would suffer some negative consequences. Norms would rise to a new level, if continuing education were given higher visibility.

All this talk about denominational requirements may sound very legalistic. But that's not the whole story. There is much more to continuing education than merely jumping through the hoops and collecting credits.

Lifelong learning is a mind-set for maximizing pastors. My research among them revealed that 91 percent are engaged in continuing education in one form or another. Away with the notion that "you can't teach an old dog new tricks." Those who would break out of the pack welcome the opportunity to learn something new. More impressive is that they often revisit an old lesson to refresh it, improve it, or rethink its validity.

It is never too soon or too late for learning. With some reluctance, I offer this personal illustration. A few years ago, it was my privilege to hear Dr. Kennon Callahan speak on the subject "A Motivational Match in Strong, Healthy Congregations." He insightfully pointed out that while the "builder" and "buster" generations usually respond to appeals on the basis of commitment, reasonability, or challenge, younger people are more likely to be motivated to action by a sense of compassion, community, or hope. It was an "aha moment." Yet the joy of learning was momentarily dampened when I realized my efforts at motivating people for years were often misguided. I had never even considered the possibility that others may not be jump-started by the same things that turn my crank. What a lesson to learn—but better late than never.

He or she who dares to teach others must never stop learning. "Let the wise listen and add to their learning, and let the discerning get guidance" (Prov. 1:5). "Instruct a wise man and he will be wiser still; teach a righteous man and he will add to his learning" (9:9).

Some of us wistfully reflect on the day when ministers were among the most respected members of the community, not in league with used car salesmen and the like. What happened? A comprehensive answer to that question could steer us far beyond the scope of this subject. A partial answer, relevant to this discussion, should include the acknowledgment that ministers are no longer the most educated individuals in most communities and the admission that other professionals often take lifelong learning more seriously.

We must heed the calls of Scripture and a changing culture. We must keep learning and growing. The knowledge and skills acquired at the outset of this adventure are not sufficient for a ministry spanning several decades. The future belongs to those who are willing to learn, unlearn, and relearn. A variety of continuing education "brokers" (colleges, seminaries, hospitals, parachurch organizations, megachurches, etc.) stand ready to provide us with tools. Delivery systems are in place. It's up to us to seize the opportunities for continuing education, lest our terminal degrees live up to their name.

FEAR OF FAILURE

In his book titled *There's a Lot More to Health than Not Being Sick,* Bruce Larson tells the story about how he and a few others were invited to try out a friend's new sailboat. A brisk breeze was blowing and the proud new owner announced, "I have been sailing for seventy years and never tipped over a sailboat!" The other men were astonished for they, too, were veteran sailors. One of them candidly responded, "You've done this for seventy years and never tipped over? I don't think you've ever really sailed." He knew that part of the fun was in the possibility of capsizing.[36]

Success always involves risk and a sense of adventure. Think for a moment. Could it be that you have been safely sailing along for years and never experienced the joy of a risk-taking adventure? Are you among the passive perfectionists whose procrastination can be traced to the fear of making mistakes? Such caution often contributes to underachievement.

Have you noticed that "think outside the box" has become the mantra from Main Street to Wall Street in today's world that seems obsessed with novelty? The Google search engine links you to 480,000 matching sites using that phrase. It is a cliché and until somebody thinks outside the box and comes up with a new phrase for thinking outside the box, we are stuck with it. It seems as if the new millennium provided just cause for virtually everyone to rethink conventional wisdom and to ask why we do the things we do. During the 1990s, we learned that paradigms were not two coins but rather new ways of looking at things, and a growing choir of voices has been singing the praises of out of the box thinking ever since.

Out of the box thinking is OK, as far as it goes. However, I am coming to believe that pastors who are serious about realizing their professional potential must embrace *out of the boat* thinking instead. There are distinct differences between the two, as a study of Matt. 14:25-33 reveals.

> During the fourth watch of the night Jesus went out to them, walking on the lake. When the disciples saw him walking on the lake, they were terrified. "It's a ghost," they said, and cried out in fear.
>
> But Jesus immediately said to them: "Take courage! It is I. Don't be afraid."
>
> "Lord, if it's you," Peter replied, "tell me to come to you on the water."
>
> "Come," he said.
>
> Then Peter got down out of the boat, walked on the water and came toward Jesus. But when he saw the wind, he was afraid and, beginning to sink, cried out, "Lord, save me!"
>
> Immediately Jesus reached out his hand and caught him. "You of little faith," he said, "why did you doubt?"
>
> And when they climbed into the boat, the wind died down. Then those who were in the boat worshiped him, saying, "Truly you are the Son of God."

John Ortberg, in the title of his book, reminds us, *If You Want to Walk on Water, You've Got to Get Out of the Boat* and insightfully points out that this passage highlights the pattern of what happens in a person that God wants to use:

- There is always a call. God asks an ordinary person to engage in an act of extraordinary trust, that of getting out of the boat.
- There is always fear. God has a habit of asking people to do things that are scary to them.
- There is always reassurance. God promises His presence and the gifts that are needed to fulfill His assignment.
- There is always a decision. People must decide whether or not to heed the call.
- There is a changed life. Those who say yes to God's call don't walk perfectly, but they learn and grow even from their failures. Those who say no are changed too—they become a little more resistant to God's calling in the future.[37]

The dialogue in this narrative is brief but meaningful. The impulsive Peter blurts out, "Lord, if it's you, tell me to come to you on the water." "Come," Jesus answers. This terse exchange underscores that getting out of the boat is more than just taking a risk; it's a matter of trust and obedience. Jesus is looking for courageous men and women who will do whatever He asks of them. Will you be among them? In Noah's day, God's message was "get into the boat"; these days, the Master says "out of the boat!"

In out of the box thinking, it's all about *good* ideas.
In out of the boat thinking, it's all about *God's* ideas.

Out of the box thinking is often conducted in the *supper* room.
Out of the boat thinking is best done in the *upper* room.

Out of the box thinking results in *Aha!* moments.
Out of the boat thinking leads to *Amen!* moments.

An out of the box mentality encourages change for *change's* sake.
An out of the boat mentality proposes change for *Christ's* sake.

Would-be wave walkers must overcome their fear of failure, a fear that has its roots in personal insecurities. Image isn't everything. Peter didn't seem to care about how his colleagues might perceive him, even if he made a fool of himself. The stage was set for humiliation—the kind of slapstick stuff you might see on *America's Funniest Home Videos.* But Peter was intent on obeying Jesus, sink or swim. Friends, we wouldn't worry so much about what others think of us if we realized how seldom they do.

Many people who haven't affirmed their intrinsic value believe that their accomplishments define their worth. This erroneous thinking creates a fear of failure. "Fear of rejection is a direct consequence of not defining your own value and lovability. You may refrain from pursuing your goals for fear of the scorn, anger, or jealousy that you could receive from others."[38]

When it comes to past failures, we have the memory of an elephant. All pastors have horror stories of the dream program that became an awful nightmare. We recall how that trial balloon for a bold, new initiative was immediately shot down by the church boss who convinced everyone that it was too expensive or too disruptive of the way they've always done it. Then, there are those times when we have simply fallen flat on our own faces. With no one to blame but ourselves, we have made a mess of things in an effort to do something different. Things do not always work out the way we had planned, and we must occasionally eat crow. As you know, the easiest way to eat crow is while it's still warm. The colder it gets, the harder it is to swallow. Just thinking back to those experiences can cause us to break out in half-dollar hives. If that's not enough, other pastors rehearse their similar stories in front of us and reinforce our fears about ever taking risks again.

"Mistakes," said James Joyce, "are the portals of discovery."[39] In the aftermath of Hurricane Katrina (our nation's most devastating natural disaster), the Federal Emergency Management Agency (FEMA) drew sharp criticism for its handling of the recovery and relief efforts in the Gulf Coast. Mistakes were made, some with deadly consequences. Hopefully, the debriefings taught federal, state, and local officials valuable lessons about how to better prepare for future storms and respond to their victims. Whenever I blew it as a pastor, informal debriefings with staff and laypersons led to some wonderful discoveries about myself, my work, my congregation, and my Master—experiential truth learned in the school of hard knocks.

Some use failure as a launching pad for future success, while others are paralyzed by it. Psychologist Perry Buffington writes about the Zeigarnik effect—what happens when our brain remembers incomplete tasks longer than completed ones. It's the stuff of sleepless nights. "Failures," says Buffington, "have no closure. The brain continues to spin the memory, trying to come up with ways to fix the mess and move it from active to inactive status."[40]

Some may argue that their church polity and rewards system have discouraged "out of the boat" thinking. Admittedly, mavericks are sometimes restricted by governing structures and viewed with suspicion when they dare to push the envelope. Even their loyalty and integrity are questioned in some circles. Whenever leaders move way out in front of the troops, they can be easily mistaken for the enemy and shot.

However, a new day is dawning. I am encouraged that nowadays "out of the boat" pastors are not just tolerated but are often celebrated for their wave walking. If innovative thinking is to become the norm, denominational officials must intentionally cultivate a climate that is favorable to change. Wave walking is never "safe"; however, judicatory leaders can make it a bit safer for the pastor who dares to step out in faith to go where few, if any, have gone before. That's exactly what happens when the emphasis is on resourcing, not regulating and restricting.

Our Win Wisconsin missional strategy, inspired by Paul Borden's book *Hit the Bullseye,* calls for rethinking the role of the district/regional leader and his or her office.[41] In this new paradigm, the district/regional leader becomes a church consultant; the district/regional office becomes a resource center. The district/regional leader meets with local lay leaders and pastors during weekend consultations devoted to assessing church health issues and encouraging helpful innovations. Agreed-upon strategies are sealed in a covenant between God, local leaders, and the district/regional leader. Here's the genius of the plan: multiple interactions with lay leaders give the district/regional leader the opportunity to clearly communicate his or her support of the pastor's fresh, new ways of doing ministry. On a parallel track, the district/regional leader requires his or her pastors to submit a monthly personal progress report that encourages out of the boat thinking through questions that zero in on processes, not outcomes. For example, each pastor is asked to describe the current activities his or her church has designed to reach out to the community rather than report on how many newcomers attended church that month. It is a subtle yet clear reminder that it's OK to have some missional failures.

In the Canadian northland toward James Bay where relatively few people live, there are just two seasons—winter and July. Extreme freezes and thaws make roadwork a monumental task, prompting officials to post this warning sign on one of the long stretches: "Be careful what rut you choose . . . you'll be in it for the next 20 miles!" Keep in mind, ruts are shallow graves. Your ministry will suffer a long and agonizing death unless you overcome the fear of failure to embrace the new thing Jesus calls you to do.

While the church's essential message remains the same, our methods must be updated in the light of our changing culture. The British created a civil service job in 1803 calling for a man to stand on the Cliffs of Dover with a spyglass. He was supposed to ring a bell if he saw Napoleon coming. The job was not abolished until 1945—just 124 years after Napoleon's death! In *Up the Organization*, Robert Townsend declares that "it's eleven times easier to start something than it is to stop it," and proposes that every organization needs an executive in charge of killing things.[42] The church is no exception. Our methods become sacred to us and they often outlive their usefulness. There is no particular virtue in doings things the way they always have been done, so let's refuse to accept status quo and call on the Author of creativity to guide us into fresh new ways of doing ministry in the 21st century.

A cursory reading of the Bible reveals that people of faith were not always faithful people. The converse is true—faithful people were not always people of faith. Enter the other disciples in the boat with Peter. Fear overcame their faith. They were really into comfort and so are we. The safety and security of the boat keeps us sailing along, content with the same-old, same-old. There is danger associated with getting out of the boat, to be sure. However, I feel compelled to remind you that there is danger in staying in it as well. If you remain in the boat, you will eventually die of boredom and stagnation. Some of you have heard the Master's voice, but fears are keeping you from obeying Him immediately. You intend to get out of the boat one of these days. You are hoping that, given time, circumstances will change and your life storms will subside, making it much easier for you to take that first step of faith. For most of us, however, one of these days is none of these days. Do not wait for perfect conditions. Remember that Jesus called Peter from the boat *during* the storm, not after it. If you throw caution to the wind and step out of the boat in response to Jesus' summons, you will enjoy the greatest adventures of your life. The greatest risk is not taking one.

Before leaving this subject, I would offer a word of caution for extreme risk-takers who would rather fail in a blaze of glory than succeed through patient effort. You know the type. In the movie *Tin Cup,* Kevin Costner plays such a character, a club professional golfer who squanders his chance to win the U.S. Open by attempting the impossible shot over water several times instead of laying up safely. My guess is that the rare pastor who engages in such self-sabotaging behavior is more concerned about making a name for himself or herself than obeying the Lord. Regardless of their motives, extreme risk-takers underachieve because of their inconsistent, reckless tactics.

A LONE RANGER MENTALITY

The call to discipleship is a call to community. We should all be grateful that it's not just "Jesus and me on the Jericho Road." Indeed, the privileges and blessings that we have in association together in the Church of Jesus Christ are very sacred and precious. Not long ago, I heard Dr. Dennis Kinlaw (former president of Asbury College) say that he would be a Christian, if for no other reason than the friends you get to meet as a result of following the Lord. I agree.

We cherish our association together, or do we? For at least two decades now, sociologists have observed a disturbing trend in which the busyness, transience, and technological advances of contemporary life seem to be undermining the sense of community among us. We are drifting apart, slowly but surely. People shun group events in favor of solitary pursuits. More and more people are living in gated communities where cocooning is commonplace. In an essay titled "Bowling Alone: America's Declining Social Capital," Robert Putnam argued that civil society is eroding because people are becoming increasingly disconnected from their neighbors. He chose bowling as the illustrative symbol, pointing out that more Americans than ever were bowling, but league participation was down 40 percent since 1980.[43]

In *Habits of the Heart*, Robert Bellah and his associates suggest that our deepest personal and societal problems can be traced to individualism. They point out that individualistic values have been glorified and glamorized by mythical heroes (the Lone Ranger, Superman, and others) who are not team players. The subtle message goes something like this: to serve society, one must be able to stand alone.[44] As pastors, far too many of us have bought into that philosophy and abandoned the traditional pattern of God mediating to us through community life. In so doing, we have limited our effectiveness.

Although *rugged* is the adjective that most often describes individualists, Lone Ranger pastors are usually rather smooth and professional. In fact, it may be that smooth professionalism that causes them to devalue a collaborative ministry. I can think of a few misunderstood geniuses who, by their arrogant demeanor, discourage lay involvement. It must have been one such leader who penned the words of this anonymous poem:

In matters controversial
My perception's very fine;
I always see both sides of things,
The one that's wrong and mine.

Lone Ranger pastors seldom train and trust others. With disregard for the clear biblical teaching about spiritual gifts in general and the pastor's equipping role in particular, they may mutter, "If you want it done right, you've got to do it yourself!" That mentality limits the scope of a church's ministry, robs willing workers of the so-called "helper's high," and grieves the heart of God. Pastor, realize your own empowerment by empowering others for meaningful works of ministry.

The most effective pastors today are the ones that are developing team-based leadership, an approach deeply rooted in Scripture and warmly received in contemporary culture. Perhaps, we should bear in mind that the two Old Testament root images that inform our consciousness of the church—*ecclesia* (a gathering of called-out ones) and *synagogue* (a congregation)—suggest that our faith is to be lived out in the context of community; moreover, the New Testament descriptions and prescriptions reinforce that point. Think about the primary images of the Church found in the Gospels and Epistles—God's people, Body of Christ, flock, family, army, a holy nation, priests, servants, and so on. These terms and a plethora of "one another" passages are clear reminders that the Church is a *community* that identifies with Christ and His mission. I would argue that the deepest sense of community arises from a group's shared commitment to mission, since communal life can only flourish if it exists for a purpose outside of itself. As God's people, the New Israel, we are *all* to be involved in His revelatory purposes in the world.

Shared ministry requires clear channels of two-way communication through which pastors and laity alike "speak the truth in love." Jim Collins's "good to great" companies had a penchant for "intense dialogue."[45] I believe that the same could be said of great churches. Here's the problem—many insecure Lone Rangers dispense information on a need-to-know basis, stifle discussion, and give the impression that their opinion is the only one that matters.

Kingdom purposes might be better served by inviting laypersons to the mission instead of challenging them to the vision. In *Life Together,* Dietrich Bonhoeffer boldly declared,

> God hates visionary dreaming; it makes the dreamer proud and pretentious. The man who fashions a visionary ideal of community demands that it be realized by God, by others, and by himself. He enters the community of Christians with his demands, sets up his own law, and judges the brethren and God Himself accordingly. . . . He acts as if he is the creator of the Christian community, as if his dream binds men together. When things do not go his way, he calls the effort a failure. When his ideal picture is destroyed, he sees the community going to smash. So he becomes first an accuser of his

brethren, then an accuser of God, and finally the despairing accuser of himself.[46]

In an effort to dictate what happens in and through the church, controlling pastors often introduce their ideas with the discussion-ending phrase "God told me . . ." and press church members to buy into the proposal. Been there—done that! Please do not misunderstand me at this point. God certainly can and often does reveal His purposes to the pastor-leader. History is replete with examples. However, we need to realize that God's vision and plans for the church are best discovered in the context of community—often channeled through or refined by Spirit-filled lay members.

The church becomes a community when *we* replaces *me*. Instead of trying to motivate everyone to buy into *my* vision, the maximizing pastor creates a climate where God's people discover *His* vision together. How do you do that? Well, the long answer to that question could become the subject of another book. Here's the short answer: lead with questions, not answers; engage in dialogue, not coercion; conduct autopsies, without blame.[47] "Touch not God's anointed" does not mean that laypersons should refrain from honest assessments of church conditions that could possibly reflect negatively on the pastor. In fact, regular assessments enhance church health and pave the way for growth in the church and its leader.

I recommend annual church board retreats for prayer, team building, assessment, and strategic planning—all those important things that tend to get replaced on the monthly agenda by urgent matters. Once the group begins to bond in a relaxed atmosphere, they will open up with honest answers to your lead questions, such as these:

- What is the unique mission of our church?
- What are our core values?
- What's going well in our work to fulfill that mission? What's not?
- Why are we doing what we are doing?
- How do you envision the church five years from now?
- What steps do we need to take now to realize that desired future?
- Should we cancel some programs that are ineffective or incongruent with our mission?

- Is God leading us to launch other ministries?
- What's the spiritual climate within the church and what can be done to improve it?

Warning—such dialogue may place you squarely on the hot seat because so much of the church's ministry was born in your heart. Out of respect for the pastoral office, some laypersons are reluctant to say anything that might injure your spirit. Encourage their honest assessments —for the good of the church and for your own development. The moment a leader gets overly defensive and allows the group to focus on his or her reactions to the assessment, the lay leaders will likely settle for status quo or worse.

The maximizing pastor builds solid relationship bridges with laypersons that enhance the ongoing dialogue of a shared ministry. Keep the conversations going. What people are not up on, they tend to be down on! Love your people unconditionally. Listen carefully to their words and the unspoken message behind those words. There's wisdom in the Cherokee saying, "Listen to the whispers and you won't have to hear the screams." Learn from them—none of us is as smart as all of us. As you love, listen, and learn, you may be able to lead your flock effectively.

Criticism often comes when we least expect it, from those who are least qualified to give it, in a form through which we are least likely to accept it. Thus, our tendency is to be dismissive with comments like— "consider the source." I challenge you to consider the criticism, not the source, and give it an honest hearing. Take the useful with the useless, like eating watermelon and spitting out the seeds. Allow critics the privilege of challenging your thoughts, with the understanding that they often say things we need to hear.

Years ago, one of my professors led our class in an exercise that proved that group decisions are better than individual ones. First, every student was asked to prioritize about 10 life-saving steps that would enable us to escape a fifth-floor hotel fire, such as calling 911, breaking the outside window, placing a towel under the door leading into the hallway, waving a sheet outside the window, and so on. Then we huddled in small groups of five or six students to discuss the order in which these steps should be taken and agreed on a plan of action. Finally, our individual and group plans for escape were compared to the official escape plan recommended by the National Safety Council. In light of their information, I would have been toast by following my instincts in an actual fire. On the other hand, the group's plan would have secured my safety. There's a lesson here. Many of our plans go up in smoke because they have never been scrutinized and refined by a group of Spirit-filled laypersons who are eager to invest themselves in cooperative ministry opportunities.

Most of us have an inflated opinion of our own ideas. Remember, however, that even our best ideas grow better when they are transplanted into someone else's mind. Do not underestimate the value of shared thinking. Dr. John Maxwell points out that a great idea is the compounding effect of a lot of good ideas, and he proposes that leaders assemble the right kind of people together for collaboration. He describes them as

> people whose greatest desire is the success of the idea; people who can compound another's thought; people who emotionally can handle the changes of conversation; people who appreciate strengths in others; people who recognize their place of value at the table; people who place what is best for them below what is best for the team; people who can bring out the best thinking in those around them; people who possess maturity, experience, and success in the issue being discussed; people who take ownership and responsibility for the decisions that are made; people who can leave the table with a we attitude and not a me attitude.[48]

At this point, some of you may be wondering, "Where is the prophetic voice in all of this consensus building?" In a room where everyone is speaking, is it ever appropriate for the pastor to declare "thus saith the Lord"? You betcha, especially on those rare occasions where one is quite certain that he or she has the mind of Christ on a given matter. However, my experience has taught me that the will of God is almost always discerned and confirmed by a group of godly lay leaders. Admittedly, most of us will sense the tension between our prophetic and consensus building roles, but it's a creative tension that should result in broader ownership to His plans for us.

NEPOTISM

The word *nepotism* derives from the Latin word *nepos,* meaning nephew. During the Middle Ages, some Catholic popes and bishops who had taken vows of chastity raised their illegitimate sons as nephews and gave them preferential treatment. The historical record reveals that several popes elevated nephews and other relatives to the cardinalate, sometimes in an effort to continue a papal dynasty. For example, Pope Callixtus III, of the Borgia family, appointed two of his nephews cardinals and one of them, Rodrigo, became Pope Alexander VI. Known as one of the most corrupt popes, Alexander proceeded to elevate Alessandro Farnese, his mistress's brother, to the position of cardinal. You guessed it—he, too, ascended to the papacy, becoming Pope Paul III. Paul kept the tradition alive by making two nephews, ages 14 and 16, cardinals. The practice of nepotism in the Catholic Church officially ended when Pope Innocent XII issued a bull in 1692. The papal bull prohibited popes from bestowing estates, offices, or revenues on any relative, with the exception that only one qualified relative could be appointed cardinal.

Nepotism, however, has made a huge comeback and continues to flourish on the contemporary scene. It is not uncommon to see the relative of a prominent political figure rise to power seemingly without the necessary qualifications. For instance, U.S. Senator Frank Murkowski, upon his election as governor of Alaska, appointed his daughter Representative Lisa Murkowski to fill the remaining two years of his term. The recent influx of the thespian offspring in the movie industry suggests that nepotism is alive and well in Hollywood. It's everywhere from Wall Street to Main Street, giving credence to the old adage that "It's not *what* you know but *who* you know that matters."

Despite nepotism's acceptance in many world areas, individualistic Americans tend to reject it outright—unless, of course, one is fortunate enough to be on the receiving end of nepotism. It seems so unfair; it smacks of injustice; it offends our sense of fair play. After all, aren't we supposed to earn what we get and not have it handed to us on a silver platter?

Some see nothing wrong with nepotism. In fact, Adam Bellow

wrote *In Praise of Nepotism*—in which he redefines it not as a "deplorable lack of public spirit" but as "the very bedrock of social existence"— a natural, healthy concern for family and, by extension, those ethnically or otherwise similar to ourselves. He argues that nepotism is a basic instinct rooted in the social biology of animals and humans, and that it may be a necessary and positive force in evolution. Ironically, the author himself is the son of novelist Saul Bellow.[49]

You need not possess a special gift of discernment to see that the church can have its share of nepotism. It is not my purpose to trace it within my Zion or yours; that's the stuff of Internet blogs and underground newsletters. I have no interest in digging up the dirt under anyone's family tree. However, I mention this delicate subject because in some cases nepotism can be a contributing factor to underachievement. Let me explain. Nepotism may allow the well-connected pastor to move up the ecclesiastical ladder with limited professional growth. That same pastor would have been more motivated to sharpen his or her skills, if there were no familial connections that virtually secured a comfortable vocational future.

Clearly there are some who lack the family ties but have mastered the fine art of schmoozing in hopes of rising through the ranks by means of their connections. The results are the same—ministry "success" despite professional mediocrity.

Let me hurry to say that this is true in some cases, not all. I believe that the majority of the connected clergy are among the best and brightest. Many are my dear friends. Our discussions leave me with the distinct impression that their firsthand exposure to their relative's ministry provided them informal educational opportunities from which they draw regularly. I would liken it to what happens when youngsters grow up in the home of a professional athlete; like Barry Bonds, many of them become great players themselves. Hanging out in the locker rooms and practice fields, these aspiring athletes learn the game inside and out. The same thing happens in almost every professional field—education, medicine, law, music, entertainment, and so on. In an osmosis-like process, kids learn the "game" from relatives and it gives them a leg up when they enter that field. Furthermore, connections provide entrée into employment and social positions unavailable to the unconnected.

I would offer words of caution to both the connected and the unconnected. If you are in a position to benefit from nepotism, guard against the temptation to coast along waiting for a bigger and better assignment that could come your way via the recommendations of influential family members and close friends. Bloom where you are planted. Continue learning from relatives and connected friends. Uphold the honor of your family name. Grow yourself forward. Be the very best you can be, for the glory of God. Move only when He opens the door and confirms His will, not a moment sooner.

If you are among the majority of unconnected pastors, guard against jealousy and cynicism. I confess to having dwelt on the inequity of nepotism during the early days of my pastoral ministry. My gaze temporarily shifted from the perfect Savior to an imperfect system. My attitude went south. The cup of joy in my soul sprang a leak as a result of jealousy. Convinced and convicted of my sin, I prayed through to victory over this matter and distanced myself from the cynics who spread their poison. "Go and do likewise," if you want to be free from the enemy's grip at this point. Bloom where you are planted. Grow yourself forward. Examine your own networking motives. Be the very best you can be, for the glory of God. Trust God, not the system, to guide you along the professional path.

NEGLECT OF THE "TEMPLE"

You and I are fearfully and wonderfully made; however, the Creator did not provide us with indestructible, maintenance-free bodies. Eugene Peterson's paraphrase of Paul's first letter to the Corinthian Church provides a clear perspective on the human body: "I need to emphasize, friends, that our natural, earthly lives don't in themselves lead us by their very nature into the kingdom of God. *Their very 'nature' is to die,* so how could they 'naturally' end up in the Life kingdom?" (1 Cor. 15:50, TM, italics added).

From the moment we are born, the process of death begins. What a sobering thought! If the body's "very 'nature' is to die," one might assume that body maintenance and care are unnecessary. Not so. Hear what the Creator has to say about this matter through the apostle Paul:

> You realize, don't you, that you are the temple of God, and God himself is present in you? No one will get by with vandalizing God's temple, you can be sure of that. God's temple is sacred—and you, remember, are the temple. . . .
>
> You know the old saying, "First you eat to live, and then you live to eat"? Well, it may be true that the body is only a temporary thing, but that's no excuse for stuffing your body with food, or indulging it with sex. Since the Master honors you with a body, honor him with your body!
>
> God honored the Master's body by raising it from the grave. He'll treat yours with the same resurrection power. Until that time, remember that your bodies are created with the same dignity as the Master's body. You wouldn't take the Master's body off to a whorehouse, would you? I should hope not. . . .
>
> Or didn't you realize that your body is a sacred place, the place of the Holy Spirit? Don't you see that you can't live however you please, squandering what God paid such a high price for? The physical part of you is not some piece of property belonging to the spiritual part of you. God owns the whole works. *So let people see God in and through your body (1 Cor. 3:16-17; 6:13-15, 19-20, TM, italics added).*

It is interesting and a bit disconcerting that we pastors, who go to such great lengths in church building maintenance, find it so easy to neglect the "temple of the Holy Spirit." We fully embrace the conviction that proper care for the temple means the avoidance of sexual immorality, alcoholic beverages, tobacco, illicit drugs, and entertainments that are subversive of the Christian ethic. No problem. In fact, we have been so careful to shun these practices that holiness has often been mistakenly defined by the don'ts.

I would be remiss, however, to address this subject without mentioning a glaring inconsistency. Is it just me or has anyone else noticed that far too many of us are fighting the battle of the bulge? In light of Paul's admonition concerning "stuffing the body with food," some of us should steer away from smorgasbords and all-you-can-eat specials. We all know that a waist is a terrible thing to mind! Nonetheless, I must kindly but insistently remind the indulgent pastor that gluttony is a deadly sin that can virtually kill one's effective ministry and lead to his or her premature demise. Right or wrong, many people make decisions about whether or not to join a certain church based partially upon the appearance of its pastor.

Having said that, my primary concern here is not so much about avoiding the harmful habits, as important as that may be; it is our general apathy toward the dos of maintaining healthy bodies—namely, eating well, exercising properly, and resting regularly. Balance is the key, as you will see in the proposed ministry model of chapter 3.

Only 53 percent of the maximizing pastors I surveyed exercise on a regular basis. I am inclined to believe that the percentage would be even lower among those who did not participate in my survey. Could it be that many of us mistake motion for exercise?

In 1865, the British Parliament passed the Locomotives and Highways Act establishing the world's first speed limits—4 miles per hour in the country and 2 miles per hour in towns and villages. The act decreed that each vehicle must be preceded by a person walking 60 yards in front and waving a red flag to warn others of the vehicle's rapid approach. By the late 1800s, doctors began to notice an increase in cases of neurasthenia, a disease characterized by exhaustion, muscle and joint pain, headaches, and poor memory or concentration levels. The source? They didn't think the human body was made to withstand travel at the speeds trains were going, and they didn't think the mind could withstand the hectic pace of the world, with its telegraphs and telephones.[50]

Groundbreaking inventions of the past century have us all moving much faster than ever before. We're quite familiar with *hurry sickness*—a condition where a person always feels short of time, performs every task quickly, and gets agitated by unexpected delays. Most pastors live and serve in the fast lane. Dr. Rick Riding's Ph.D. dissertation research revealed that the pastor's average workweek is more than 62 hours and involves approximately 255 separate tasks.[51] When you ask your colleagues how they're doing these days, the answer more often than not is "busy!" We seem to have adopted James Dean's "drive fast and die young" philosophy.

The urgency of our lives becomes quite apparent when we are forced to momentarily put life "on hold." This is especially true when it comes to waiting for elevators. We respond to these momentary delays by frantically pressing the button several times in an effort to transmit urgency to the elevator's brain. Elevator engineeers have devised a method to lower our anxiety level and prolong the life span of the call buttons. "Japan has pioneered another feature, called 'psychological waiting time lanterns.' As soon as someone presses a call button, a computer determines which car will reach the floor first and lights the appropriate signal well in advance of its arrival. This gives the illusion of an instantaneous response and, as a side benefit, herds riders into position for quick loading."Once on board, our frustration intensifies as we wait another 2-4 seconds for the door to close.[52] Why do we get visibly upset by such minor delays? Simply because waiting interrupts our doing.

Yes, we live in a world where people speed walk along moving sidewalks in the airport and the slightest delay when the traffic light turns green prompts a horn-blowing rage by dashboard diners behind you. This need for speed takes a devastating toll on our health. Beware, lest we be lulled into thinking that we are getting proper exercise just because our pace has quickened. The American College of Sports Medicine recommends cardiovascular workouts three to five days per week, 30 to 60 minutes per session, for significant cardiorespiratory and fat-burning benefits. If you are really out of shape, perhaps you should start with the couch potato workout designed and promoted by the American Physical Therapy Association. Although the names of the six exercises are tongue-in-cheek references to football, they are all designed to work a large variety of muscles without having to leave your television—the Couch Potato Kick Off Lateral Leg Lift, Hail Mary Back and Arm Extensor, Touch Back Wall Squats, Soda Stretch Side Bend, Bad Call Neck Rotation, and Second Half Bent-Knee Hamstring Stretch.[53] Seriously, go exercise and have fun.

At the end of the day, you'll need your rest. "No one, not even CEOs, are resistant to the effects of sleep loss," says J. Catesby Ware, professor of Eastern Virginia Medical School and director of the Sleep Disorders Center at Sentara Norfolk General Hospital. "Sleep-deprived people can perform routine tasks; however, they are less likely to come up with novel or the most appropriate decisions."[54] Research reveals that if you want to be healthy and creative, you need seven to nine hours of sleep per night. Even short-term lack of sleep negatively impacts your hormone levels, heart rate, mood, and memory. Sorry, sleep camels, you cannot make up for it by sleeping late on Saturday.

Ours is an adrenaline-intensive profession, and modern science warns of the damage that can occur when stressful stimuli are not interrupted by cyclical rest—the kind of Sabbath rest described and prescribed in the Word. Eighty percent of the maximizing pastors reported a regular day off—it should be 100 percent. If you need more convincing, I suggest that you read Dr. Dan Spaite's *Time Bomb in the Church: Defusing Pastoral Burnout*. And remember Peter Wagner's quote worth requoting: "If you're a good pastor, every year you need a vacation. If you're a bad pastor, every year your congregation needs a vacation!"[55]

BRIEF TENURE

Neighborhoods across the country are littered with For Sale signs. Although relocation was rather rare just a generation or two ago, today approximately 16 percent of all Americans move within any given year and 33 percent of all renters.[56] Roots do not grow as deeply as they once did. A comprehensive explanation for society's transience would include several underlying sociological factors, the greatest of which may be the tenuous relationship that exists between American workers and their employers. Gone are the days when one might expect to work at the same place for a lifetime. Amid downsizing and restructuring, countless corporations have demonstrated a lack of commitment to their employees. As a result, worker loyalty has diminished to the point where now the average American worker is expected to hold eight different jobs by his or her 40th birthday.

Everyone moves more often these days, including ministers. In fact, since the mid 1970s pastoral tenure has dropped from an average of 7 years per church to about 5 years. The younger the pastors are, the shorter their average tenure. A surprising 8 percent of pastors under 40 years of age have moved 10 or more times, averaging between 1 and 2 years per church.[57] Barna's research revealed that the typical pastor has the greatest ministry impact at a church during years 5 through 14.[58] The word must be spreading because some denominations that have traditionally moved their clergy every few years are reconsidering that practice.

Barna's findings square with my personal experience and unscientific observations. You need to understand that I am a sprinter, not a marathon runner. I hit the ground running. Even so, it took me a year or so to get acquainted and fall in love with the church members. By the end of the second year, I usually possessed a pretty good understanding of congregational culture (history, spiritual climate, resources, communication issues, core values, key influencers, decision-making processes, barriers to growth, etc.). Exegeting the surrounding community was a bit more difficult, often taking several years to truly get a grip on the needs of the people in our mission field. During the third year, with a few wins under the belt, I sensed that most members began to trust my leadership and were ready to move together with me into mission. You have to live with integrity among your people for quite a while before positional leadership becomes truly authoritative and effective. Once leadership capital was built up, I was careful to spend it wisely. While we experienced some great victories early on, our most fruitful period was year four and beyond. I regret leaving pastorates too soon on at least two occasions. Please be careful not to make that same mistake. If you do not sense God's clear release from an assignment, stay long enough to enjoy the fruit of your labors in those first few years.

Pastors move for various reasons; some do so against their will. If you've ever left a pastorate under duress, you may be able to identify with Woody Hayes, the legendary Ohio State football coach. In response to being offered a car a couple of times, he quipped, "You know how that works. They give you the Cadillac one year, and the next year they give you the gas to get out of town." Yes, those who are singing your praises one day may be encouraging your departure the next day. It occurs to me that "Jesus knows all about our struggles" at that point. Obviously, you cannot remain in an assignment where local and judicatory leaders have gone through the proper procedures to remove you. You can, however, take the high road out of town and avoid further injury to the Body of Christ.

More often than not, pastors leave on their own terms and too soon. While it's true that *how* one serves is more important than *how long*, both determine the effectiveness of our ministry. To some degree, we are all products of our environment and much of our restlessness can be traced to society's mobility. And let's face it—there's something very attractive about fresh faces and fresh places. Eugene Peterson warns against "ecclesiastical pornography," fantasizing about a glamorous church without spots or wrinkles.[59] Sure, the grass always seems greener on the other side; just keep in mind, however, there may be a septic tank below it!

According to Frederick Buechner, "The place God calls you is the place where your deep gladness and the world's deep hunger meet."[60] I would hasten to add that "your deep gladness" doesn't necessarily mean that your ministry will be a nonstop source of joy each and every step of the way. Even strong families can have disagreements; winners get wounded in the battle. Emotions ebb and flow. The Bible is filled with examples of those who found themselves in unhappy ministerial situations—Moses, Elijah, Jeremiah, Jonah, Paul, and even Jesus all came to a point where they cried out, "I can't take it anymore!" Did God release them from the assignment? No. Loosely translated, His answer was, "You can make it. Hang in there. I will help you."

Many of us can testify that our "deep gladness" was intensified when God gave us strength to keep on keeping on. It may encourage some of you to know that God honored my perseverance in one place with significant church growth and a new building, after a congregational vote that nearly led to my premature departure. During some difficult days there, I phoned a district superintendent friend in hopes that he would ease my pain with a call to a kinder, gentler church. Instead, he gave me something better—the wisdom of these words: "Stay put. . . . you'll do your best holiness preaching in the way you respond to your critics." I did and, in so doing, learned a valuable lesson—fight or flight are not the only two options for a pastor under fire. It just might be right to sit tight and shed His light in the dark night.

A sportswriter once asked Bob Uecker, "How did you handle pressure as a professional baseball player?" The witty one replied, "It was easy, I'd strike out and put the pressure on the guy behind me." There's pressure in our game. Don't strike out; don't bail out; don't put pressure on the guy behind you. Stay put. The God who called you to that tough assignment will strengthen you in it. Far too often, when the going gets tough, the tough get going—out of town.

Long-term pastorates stretch us professionally. You have to grow, if you remain in a church for an extended period of time. Recycled sermons and lessons will barely keep the folk awake, much less make disciples of them. The same-old, same-old stuff pales in comparison to the dynamic ministry taking place just down the road from you. The statistics make me believe that the majority of us have opted for a 4-year ministry in five different places, rather than experiencing the deep gladness that comes along with 20 years of growing forward in the same setting.

During the sixth century when monks were on the move in search of a better monastery and holier brothers and sisters, Benedict introduced the vow of stability—stay where you are. I am not proposing that pastors take such a vow; however, I am offering a few practical suggestions that may encourage longer pastorates.

- We must intensify our efforts to improve relationships between clergy and laypersons. Church boards and newly elected or appointed pastors should clearly communicate goals and expectations with each other to avoid misunderstandings at the outset. Because those first few honeymoon weeks are critical to a lengthy marriage, we must be more scrupulous with the written understandings.

- Every pastor and church board should cultivate a climate where they can be totally transparent with each other at all times, not just during the regular church/pastoral review.

- It may be time to consider tangible, compensation incentives for the pastor, such as increased contributions toward the pastor's re-tirement fund based upon years of service rendered in the same local church. I am aware of several churches where this is already happening and, not surprisingly, this practice has resulted in the desired outcomes. To avoid rewarding mediocrity, lay leaders should probably add fruitfulness to the incentive equation.

Here is a point at which we can and should be countercultural. Let's buck the trend. I invite you to experience the joyful satisfaction of longer, more fruitful pastorates. It's a win-win situation for both the church and its leader.

MODEST COMPENSATION PACKAGES

I cannot think of anyone who entered the pastoral ministry with il-lusions of amassing great wealth. We work long hours, despite modest compensation packages, because we view ministry as a calling, not merely a career. In fact, only 1 in 10 of us would definitely or probably take a well-paying secular job, if offered one.[61]

It is virtually impossible to find *current* figures on salary packages; however, the Barna Research Group determined that the average an-nual compensation for Protestant pastors in the United States finally broke the $40,000 mark back in 2002—an increase of 25 percent since 1992. As expected, the compensation given to pastors varies significant-ly based upon the size of their church. Pastors in churches that have less than 100 adults in weekly worship attendance—a group that repre-sents the majority of the nation's congregations—receive compensation valued at $31,613 annually. In churches that attract 100 to 250 adults, the pastoral compensation package is approximately 50 percent more—$47,368 annually. The nation's largest churches (250 or more adults) pay their pastor an average of $58,333 per year. Pastors of urban and suburban churches average about one-third more each year than their rural peers.[62] Interestingly, "connectional churches" (Methodist, Luther-an, Episcopal, Presbyterian, etc.) pay considerably more than "congre-gational churches" (Baptist, Pentecostal, Disciples, United Church of Christ, etc.). According to a 2004 report, the average total compensa-tion package of a Nazarene pastor is less than $35,000.[63] Compared with other professionals with similar education and responsibilities, pastors are grossly underpaid. For instance, the salaries of corporate managers are 38 percent higher than the pastoral average; computer engineers are 63 percent higher, public school administrators are 88 percent higher, and physicians are 385 percent higher. And yet, most pastors feel they are paid fairly—68 percent to be exact.[64]

By the way, the term *salary* comes from the Latin *salarium*—a ration of salt that was given to Roman soldiers as wages. The salt was used in the preservation of food. In time, the method of payment changed to an allowance of money for the purchase of salt and eventually payment for work undertaken, or salary. Thus to be "worth one's salt" is to deserve a salary.

OK, so what's the point? How do meager wages contribute to underachievement? I run the risk of offending some of you in my answer to these questions, so please hear me out and keep in mind that I am your advocate, not your adversary. Feel free to dismiss my explanation, if it doesn't apply to you. My hunch is that the vast majority of you should not own any guilt at this point because you are providing lots of bang for the buck. However, I theorize that some of us have either consciously or subconsciously allowed a meager compensation package to justify mediocre professional performance. If we are not very careful, poor pay can generate "stinkin' thinkin'," especially when we feel overworked and underappreciated. It's an occupational hazard. The enemy gets us to entertain negative thoughts like these: "What can they expect for $200 a week?" "My teenager makes more money flipping burgers under the Golden Arches." "The church is like every other place; you get what you pay for." "If they paid me as much as Pastor Smith makes over at First Church, then I would fish less and keep better office hours." While few pastors have actually verbalized such thoughts and feelings (except to a spouse), most of us have probably been there emotionally at some point in our ministry. Don't dwell there, because feelings often dictate actions.

Once our attitude sours, the attending behaviors follow. It becomes easier and easier for one to justify laziness, shoddy administration, prepackaged Internet sermons, inconsistent shepherding, the same old programs, and much more. Poor performance yields poor results and poorer pay. It's a downward spiral. On the other hand, the pastor who accepts poor pay with a positive attitude and does his or her best will usually see positive results and receive better pay. The faulty assumption is that better pay would necessarily result in better performance. Not so. Attitude is the difference maker. Most maximizing pastors give me the impression that they would do what they do without a salary. Passion, not a paycheck, should drive us. If money is a primary motivation for peak performance, you should probably consider another line of work to avoid being frustrated for the rest of your life.

Again, it's my hunch that much of the negativity surrounding meager compensation flies below our radar, on the subconscious level. My reflections on this subject are intended to raise your awareness, not your anxiety level.

Some suggest that pastors should speak up for a fair salary, citing James 4:2 ("Ye have not, because ye ask not" [KJV]) for biblical justification. Not me. If your compensation is not what it could and should be, talk with the Lord about it; after all, the NIV says, "You do not have, because you do not ask *God"* (italics mine). I would recommend that you accept it with thanks, solicit the superintendent's assistance in educating the board in this matter, get their blessing on part-time tentmaking employment (if necessary), embrace a positive attitude, engage in missional ministry marked by excellence, and enjoy the fruit of your labor. In so doing, you'll demonstrate that you are indeed worth your salt.

AN UNSUPPORTIVE SPOUSE

Debbie and I are a team of two, equally committed to fulfilling God's purposes for our lives. Those who have known us across the years will tell you that I married way over my head. I would agree. We have been inseparable from the moment we first met at Trevecca Nazarene College. My journal entry for that day, January 16, 1971, reads:

Tonight I reluctantly attended a meeting in Bud Robinson Hall . . . actually it was supper in the school's cafeteria. Some were feeding their faces; others were feeding their minds. I'm not sure if there were any religion majors reading Luther's *Preface to the Epistle to Romans.*

About a quarter before six, while flirting with a cute co-ed, I felt my heart strangely warmed and sensed that I, even I, could fall in love.

After we had steadily dated for a few months and hinted at marriage, Debbie confided that she had felt a call to be a pastor's wife for several years. We tied the knot in June 1973 and soon thereafter started on the joyful journey that led us into five pastorates and the district superintendency. The Berkners are two hearts beating as one, and yet Debbie's identity has never been submerged into mine. In each of our ministry settings, Debbie has served alongside me as office secretary/office manager—an assignment that fits her spiritual gifts mix and personality like a tailored suit. It's been fun to see God working through her in various volunteer roles, including Sunday School teacher, children's and teen Bible quiz director, choir member and director, women's ministry coordinator, assimilation coordinator, and greeter. Her "find a need and fill it" mentality explains the countless hours invested in grunt work during two major building programs. If you were to look up the word *helpmate* in the dictionary, you just may find her picture. It would be impossible for me to overstate Debbie's positive effect upon my life and ministry.

Virtually all of the maximizing pastor respondents (98 percent) feel that their spouses strongly support their ministry. While only 25 percent of these ministry mates view their ecclesiastical work as a calling, almost all of them play an active role in the life of the local church and enjoy being a pastoral spouse—despite the pressures, loneliness, and challenges that come with the territory. Only 3 of the 149 respondents cited a partner's negative feelings concerning the ministry life. Sixty-three percent of the maximizing pastor spouses are employed; the majority work full-time; 14 percent of them are on the payroll of the local church or affiliated schools, day cares, and so on.

Static categories such as homemaker, helpmate, or career person do not serve us very well in describing the typical spouse of a maximizing pastor, and it is not my intention to endorse any of these three models, all of which hold enormous potential for satisfaction and frustration. One style does not fit all. Stay-at-home pastoral spouses certainly are the exception, not the rule, thanks to sociological shifts and the sheer economic realities related to pastoral pay. Most seem to be choosing the role or combination of roles that fit the various stages of one's life, particularly when children are a consideration. Unfortunately, some congregations expect two for the price of one—a pastor plus the spouse who provides a second income, keeps things running smoothly at home, and serves as an unpaid vocational associate. Obviously, that's a recipe for frustration and failure.

Pastors' spouses, whether they like it or not, are an extension of their husband's or wife's ministry and can be his or her greatest blessing or worst hindrance. Speaking specifically to pastors' wives, H. B. London wrote, "Unfortunately, and even unfairly, the impression you make on a congregation can greatly impact the effectiveness of your husband's ministry."[65] The same could be said of a pastor's husband. Shepherds whose spouses feel negatively toward their own role may experience difficulty even finding and keeping a church. This explains, at least in part, why the vast majority of the respondents to my survey and others like it express such delight with the assignment. Think about it—many of those who were frustrated, angry, and disillusioned are currently unassigned or divorced—making it difficult, if not impossible, for anyone to report their negative feelings. By the way, the divorce rate among clergy is higher than almost every other professional group, including lawyers and doctors.

We can easily see how an unsupportive spouse contributes to underachievement in the dropout cases; however, it may be more difficult to discern the negative impact of ministry mates who do not fully embrace the pastoral life but remain in it. Consider these possible scenarios:

- The jealous spouse who resents the church, the "pastor's mistress," for taking him away from the family too often.
- The nest-building spouse who absolutely will not move away from his or her family, despite the fact that such a move may be God's will.
- The career spouse who, after spending too much time and energy in professional pursuits, has nothing left for Kingdom interests through the local church.
- The dutiful spouse who volunteers to do anything and everything

around the church and, in the process, robs others of meaningful ministry opportunities.

- The sloppy spouse whose housekeeping habits become a stumbling block to opening up the pastor's home for the ministry of hospitality.
- The overcompensating spouse who covers the weaknesses of his or her partner without encouraging that person's growth.
- The shopping spouse whose passion for fashion has created an economic hardship on the family.
- The unkempt spouse whose personal appearance makes the pastor more vulnerable to inappropriate relationships.

If God has blessed you with a supportive ministry partner who has found favor in your eyes and in the eyes of your congregation, thank Him for this most precious gift. Do not take your spouse for granted. I would encourage you to stop reading long enough to express your love and appreciation for that special someone with whom you share the pastoral journey. It's a difficult and demanding role; she or he deserves your praise.

If your ministry mate is struggling and unwittingly contributing to your professional underachievement, I would suggest that you lovingly engage her or him in dialogue at this point—being very careful not to point an accusatory finger. It's a difficult and demanding role; she or he deserves your patience and understanding. Share your real feelings and encourage the same from your spouse. Consider the various options related to striking the proper balance between personal and professional responsibilities. Allow your spouse the space to prayerfully determine how to approach each phase of life. At the end of the day, you may need the guidance of a well-trained Christian counselor. You should begin to see some positive changes *in* your spouse without a change *of* spouses; however, the process will likely involve significant changes in *you*. Be prepared for negotiated compromise.

"The devil dances with glee," says Joyce Williams, "when a pastoral team's effectiveness is diminished."[66] Let's sit him down by renewing our romance for each other and the cause of Christ.

THREE

A 1st-Century Model for 21st-Century Ministry

Good pastors are painfully aware of the cognitive dissonance between reality (the way things are) and potential (the way things could be). We sense the need for professional development and set out on a seemingly endless search for something that will scratch where we are itching. That's why our bookshelves are bending under the weight of all those church growth and leadership conference notebooks, conveniently placed next to the latest offerings from a host of business management gurus. Yes, we desire to grow forward. Instead, far too many of us are merely becoming the products of the latest seminar we have attended or the most recent book we have read. Something is missing. That "something" is a pastoral theology that is so deeply rooted and grounded in Scripture that it cannot be swept away by the strong winds of the most current fads in the corporate or church world.

Pastors are called into *Christian* ministry, not religious work. It stands to reason, then, that we should avoid caving into the culture and approach ministry as Jesus Christ did. After all, we are committed to continuing His work. Luke introduces Acts with a reference to his "former book," the Gospel narrative in which he details "all that Jesus *began* to do and to teach until the day he was taken up to heaven, after giving instructions through the Holy Spirit to the apostles he had chosen" (Acts 1:1-2, italics added). As you know, he then proceeds to share the incredible 28-chapter account of what Jesus *continued* to do through His Spirit-filled followers. Friends, there is a real sense in which the Book of Acts is still being written today because His work goes on through us.

Jesus Christ then becomes for us the ministry model above all others, the pastoral prototype—the perfect personification of the maximizing ministry principles proposed in this book. Out of His life and ministry emerges a pastoral theology that will enable us to glorify God in truly *Christian* ministry. Since all truth is God's truth, we can certainly learn a lot from the so-called experts in various fields; however, I am convinced that we need to tarry longer at the feet of Jesus, carefully study His life and teachings, and intentionally embrace His style of ministry.

I must have decided to resign at least a hundred times during 28 years of pastoral ministry—usually on Mondays. There's no reasonable explanation for the timing. Perhaps, it is related to the psychological letdown after Sunday's "high," or maybe the Carpenters were onto something when they sang about the downside of "rainy days and Mondays." At any rate, I would like you to think of today as a Monday (if it's not) and resign religious work in favor of *Christian* ministry—that is to say, countercultural ministry that flows directly from our identification with the Christ. Who knows . . . the ministry that you've dreamed *of* just may be the ministry Jesus dreamed *up*. I propose a Christ-centered, 1st-century model for 21st-century ministry.

BIBLICAL FOUNDATIONS

Christian pastoral theology must be biblically based and, because of its very nature, particularly informed by the Gospel narratives. I have chosen to highlight six passages that, in my opinion, capture the essence of Jesus' countercultural way of doing ministry. A key concept rises from each of the following exegetical studies. Some may be surprised to learn that I have not explored authenticity as a mark of the Master's ministry; that's only because there seems to be no particular passage that illuminates it, and my chosen methodology involving exegetical study dictated this omission. I would hasten to say that the sum total of Jesus' entire life and ministry testify to His authenticity. The fulfilled prophecies, an empty tomb, eyewitness accounts, miracles, and transformed lives all confirm His claims. He was indeed who He claimed to be—God's Son, Savior of the world. If we are to have a *Christian* ministry in a world where jaded leadership is fast becoming the norm, we must abhor hypocrisy and remove our professional masks to simply be who we say we are. Maximizing pastors are the real deal—genuine, trustworthy, and reliable. With authenticity as a given, let us explore the following passages with an eye for other dominant themes and characteristics of Jesus' ministry. I believe that they are both *descriptive* and *prescriptive*.

Key Concept: Servanthood

Jesus called them together and said, "You know that those who are regarded as rulers of the Gentiles lord it over them, and their high officials exercise authority over them. Not so with you. Instead, whoever wants to become great among you must be your servant, and whoever wants to be first must be slave of all. For even the Son of Man did not come to be served, but to serve, and to give his life as a ransom for many" (Mark 10:42-45).

You recall that Jesus' words were spoken in response to the brazen request of James and John: "Let one of us sit at your right and the other at your left in your glory" (v. 37). Like most Jews of that day, they had a distorted understanding of the Messiah's kingdom and were probably thinking in terms of an earthly reign that would free Israel from Roman domination. James and John wanted honored places in it. With references to the cup and baptism, metaphors for suffering and being plunged into calamity respectively, Jesus taught them that greatness is achieved through service and graciously denied their request. The other 10 were angry with James and John for trying to get a leg up on them. Therefore, Jesus called all of them together and, in the words of our printed text, redefined greatness in terms of servanthood.

Ministry in its purest and simplest form is serving others. According to Jesus, our ministry model, the path of greatness is one of service to those around you. He drives the point home by using himself as an example, stating that he "did not come to be served, but to serve, and to give his life as a ransom for many" (v. 45). While the Cross event was the ultimate expression of servanthood, Jesus also practiced what He preached on that day when He washed the disciples' dirty feet.

In the aftermath of the 9/11 terrorist attacks, Americans began to rethink what it means to be a real hero. Who merits that moniker? Prior to that "terrible Tuesday," most of the great American heroes were celebrities—movie or TV stars, professional athletes, the rich and famous. Things are different now. Fifteen hundred New York City police officers, firefighters, and other emergency personnel have expanded our understanding of heroes to include those whose names will never appear in lights and yet go far beyond the call of duty to the point of ultimate sacrifice.

I was particularly moved by the story of Father Mychal Judge, a chaplain of the New York City Fire Department who put himself in harm's way to minister to those trapped in the collapsing Twin Towers. He was killed while comforting the dying. Father Judge and all those rescue workers are among my heroes now because of their brave demonstration of selflessness. They laid down their lives for someone else and that, according to Jesus, is the best expression of love. He said, "Greater love has no one than this, that he lay down his life for his friends" (John 15:13).

Self-giving pastors top my list of heroes. Most of you will never become ministry martyrs by losing your life in the line of duty. A word of caution: you may come dangerously close to the ultimate sacrifice by pushing too hard for changes in worship style, service times, or the church name! Nonetheless, from my perspective, you are an unheralded hero because you lay down your life in daily acts of selflessness directed toward people who may or may not recognize the sacrificial and sacramental nature of your work.

I once joined four men who were charged with the assignment of moving the church's grand piano from the platform, in preparation for our Easter drama. There wasn't a strong, healthy back in the group, but we were determined to do the job—even if it killed us. It almost did. When it became obvious that we had bit off more than we could chew, I looked around for help and summoned the pianist to assist us. "Not with these hands," he replied while walking away. To be fair, I should tell you that he was an accomplished musician whose livelihood depended upon the tools of his trade. Nevertheless, his unwillingness to use his hands did not sit well with me or the other men who desperately needed help that day. Pastors, we have a choice between a "not with these hands" attitude or one that says, "Take my hands, and let them move / At the impulse of Thy love."

The call to servanthood is countercultural, since most businesses and organizations measure greatness by outstanding personal achievements. The term *servanthood leadership* sounds like an oxymoron in a world where status-seekers step all over each other to climb to the top of the proverbial ladder and dictatorial managers declare that "it's my way or the highway!" Moreover, it has become more difficult than ever to maintain the servant spirit in church circles where increasingly larger numbers of Christians seem to prefer the charismatic, superpastor style. Dare to be different. Jesus did. Like Him, maximizing pastors are comfortable with the towel and basin.

Key Concept: Obedience

His mother said to the servants, "Do whatever he tells you." Nearby stood six stone water jars, the kind used by the Jews for ceremonial washing, each holding from twenty to thirty gallons. Jesus said to the servants, "Fill the jars with water"; so they filled them to the brim. Then he told them, "Now draw some out and take it to the master of the banquet." They did so, and the master of the banquet tasted the water that had been turned into wine (John 2:5-9).

If anything *can* go wrong, it *will* go wrong at a wedding! Murphy is never on the guest list, but he usually shows up. The setting for this passage is a wedding reception that took place soon after Jesus assembled His team of followers. They were there—and so was Murphy. The caterer underestimated the crowd, so they ran out of refreshments. Mary nudges a somewhat reluctant Jesus into public ministry and in this simple statement suggests that obedience is the key to miracles— "Do whatever he tells you" (v. 5). Jesus directed the servants to fill the jars with water, and they obeyed to the nth degree. Upon His direction, they drew a sample and took it to the master of the banquet who insisted that the bridegroom had saved the best for last. Jesus met an immediate need, revealed His glory, inspired faith among the disciples, and set the pattern for how He would work with others in the future.

It may be too much to say that the first of Jesus' miracles is prototypical; however, it should be noted that John's Gospel contains accounts of several episodes in which He cooperated with others in performing the miraculous. For example, Jesus enlisted help when He fed the multitude with the boy's lunch, raised Lazarus from the dead, and orchestrated a huge catch of fish. My point here is simply this: if you will obediently "do whatever he tells you," there's a strong possibility that the partnership with Jesus will result in something miraculous. Don't misunderstand me. Jesus could have done all these things by himself and, in fact, did act alone in performing miracles on a few occasions; however, He usually chose to involve others in the process.

In my opinion, John's narrative of Jesus' miracles goes a long way toward demystifying how Christ builds His Church. Sure, Jesus said, "I will build my church," but we seem to have overlooked His quickly adding that He was giving the "keys of the kingdom" to Peter and presumably those who followed his lead in declaring the Lordship of Christ. Some say that the "keys of the kingdom" represent the authority to carry out church discipline, legislation, and administration; others say that the keys give the authority to pronounce forgiveness of sins. I believe that the keys represent our opportunity to bring people to the Kingdom by sharing the good news of salvation. In other words, Jesus never intended to build His Church alone.

None of us would dare say that His plan for Kingdom expansion doesn't include us; yet at times we act as though we believe that. The pattern prayer rolls easily off our tongues, especially the part where we say, "Thy kingdom come. Thy will be done in earth, as it is in heaven" (Matt. 6:10, KJV). We would do well to supplement the Lord's Prayer with this request attributed to Sir Thomas More, the Renaissance author and Catholic martyr: "The things, good Lord, that we pray for, give us the grace to labor for." Think of it this way—you and Christ are working together as a dynamic duo in building His Church. "Pray as though everything depended on God; work as though everything depended on you" (Augustine). Be careful, however, not to jump the gun and get out in front of Him.

Jesus practiced what He preached, leading a life of absolute obedience to the Father's will. The Son of Man, possessing His own free will, could have taken an easier path—as He was tempted to do in the desert (4:1-11). He did not. If anyone was ever purpose-driven, it was Jesus Christ. God's plan for the salvation of the world called for His death on the Cross, and Jesus resolutely committed himself to that end. On the occasion when the disciples insisted that He eat something, Jesus replied, "My food . . . is to do the will of him who sent me and to finish his work" (John 4:34). What a meaningful metaphor. In response to the Jews who charged Jesus with "making himself equal with God" (5:18), He said, "By myself I can do nothing; I judge only as I hear, and my judgment is just, for I seek not to please myself but him who sent me" (v. 30). He echoes this same sentiment in the "bread of life" (6:35) conversation with His disciples: "For I have come down from heaven not to do my will but to do the will of him who sent me" (v. 38). Even in the Garden of Gethsemane, despite asking that the cup of suffering be taken away, Jesus reaffirmed His obedience to the will of His Father.

Sadly, too many pastors settle for congregational maintenance and rarely experience the thrill of boldly doing God's will. Our work, to be authentically *Christian,* must be marked by absolute obedience to the Master. It's a dance with the divine; He leads, we follow. Like the servants at the wedding feast, let us do whatever He tells us—even when His instructions seem ridiculous in the eyes of reason or leave us feeling totally inadequate. Whatever is to be done at God's command may be accomplished in His strength.

How can we bring ourselves to that position of total obedience and abandonment of self-will? It is not easy because it is so countercultural. When almost everyone around us has joined Frank Sinatra in singing "My Way," it takes courage to go against the flow and declare, "We will do it His way." Such trust is possible inasmuch as we remember that the Christ of infallible wisdom and infinite love cannot lead us astray. "Perfect obedience would be perfect happiness if only we had perfect confidence in the power we were obeying."[1]

Jesus linked obedience to fruitfulness in the classic vine and branches discourse in which He declared, "You are my friends if you do what I command. . . . You did not choose me, but I chose you and appointed you to go and bear fruit" (15:14, 16). The clear implication is that our fruitfulness hinges upon our willingness to obey Jesus and cooperate with Him in a miraculous work. It is a sobering truth that our free will can thwart the will of God. As crazy as it may seem, God has restricted His own omnipotence by creating free creatures who may or may not cooperate with Him in the accomplishment of His purposes. If this idea makes you a bit uncomfortable, I would remind you that the Lord himself was not able to do miracles in some places because the people's faith was absent.

Jesus' parabolic teaching about the wise and foolish builders (Luke 6:46-49) reminds us that some who call Him Lord do not do what He says. On occasion, I have been among them and so have you; however, we have cleverly masked our disobedience by labeling it caution. Few of us would dare to shake our fist in the face of God shouting, "I will not"; instead, we bargain with God and say, "I will, but not now" and ease our consciences with the idea that this is not refusal. "You may have been duped into believing that being extremely 'cautious' is a sign of wisdom, stability, and maturity, when in reality it *may* be nothing more than disobedience in disguise."[2] Delay is disobedience. Let us come to Jesus, hear His words, and put them into practice—so that our "house" (ministry) will withstand the floods.

Key Concept: Excellence

Jesus commanded them not to tell anyone. But the more he did so, the more they kept talking about it. People were overwhelmed with amazement. "He has done everything well," they said. "He even makes the deaf hear and the mute speak" (Mark 7:36-37).

In this healing narrative, Mark tells us very little about the man or his friends. We only know that they brought "a man who was deaf and could hardly talk" (v. 32) to Jesus, in hopes that He would place healing hands upon their friend. Apparently, Jesus' reputation preceded Him. In a rather unorthodox manner, Jesus restored the man's hearing and loosened his tongue so that he could speak plainly. Oddly, Jesus commanded them to keep quiet about what He had done. Instead, they kept buzzing about it and, in the words of the printed text, praised Jesus as the One who "has done everything well" (v. 37)—echoing the words of Gen. 1:31 regarding God's work in creation. Jesus' healing here represents God's way of doing "everything well."

Excellence was one of the more popular buzzwords of the 1980s and 1990s—thanks, in large measure, to the popularity of *In Search of Excellence* written by Thomas J. Peters and Robert H. Waterman Jr.[3] Several authors followed suit. Like so many other good terms, *excellence* lost some of its punch because of overexposure. In fact, a pastor friend informed me recently that generation Xers are looking for authenticity, not excellence, in ministry. That's too bad. Oh, I'm all for authenticity, but not at the expense of excellence. They are not mutually exclusive virtues. It's a matter of both-and not either-or.

Let me explain. Jesus was the most authentic human being to ever walk the face of this earth; He was as real as real can be. No mask; no pretense. Nothing plastic about Him. When you are God, why try to be anyone else! And yet the genuine Jesus performed ministry that was characterized by excellence—so much so that the onlookers likened the quality of His work to that of God the Creator. "He has done everything well," they said. What a commendation.

Can you see why I bristle a bit when someone dismisses excellence, as if it were some passing fad that went out with the Rubik's Cube? *Excellence* isn't a buzzword whose time has come and gone. It is a key component to *Christian* ministry, without which one dishonors the Christ in whose name we serve.

It is much easier to identify excellence than define it. Sometimes the best way to describe something is to first clarify what it is not. Excellence is not perfect performance. Aren't you pleased about that? People do dumb things. My life provides some remarkable examples of ineptitude, including the time when I addressed the Lord as "Honey" during an altar call prayer! Even when we are doing our best to get it right, our humanity shines through.

Excellence should not be mistaken for success. Unfortunately, excellence has been closely connected to success theology and prostituted by those who viewed it as a ticket to acquire success and the wealth, power, and prestige that come with it. Jon Johnston offers these insightful observations:

> Success offers a hoped-for future goal; excellence provides a striven-for present standard. Success bases our worth on a comparison with others; excellence gauges our value by measuring us against our own potential. Success grants its rewards to the few, but is the dream of the multitudes; excellence is available to all living beings, but is accepted by the special few. Success focuses its attention on the external—becoming the tastemaker for the insatiable appetites of the conspicuous consumer; excellence beams its spotlight on the internal spirit—becoming the quiet, but pervasive, conscience of the conscientious who yearn for integrity. . . . Success encourages expedience and compromise, which prompt us to treat people as means to our ends; excellence cultivates principles and consistency, which ensure that we will treat all persons as intrinsically valuable ends—the apex of our heavenly Father's creation.[4]

The Greek word for excellence, *aretē*, connotes virtue, superiority, preeminence, and even perfection. R. W. Livingstone sheds more light on the term's meaning:

It is the belief that man is more important than his environment or his possessions, and that his fundamental business is not to understand nature, though this is one of his problems, nor to earn a livelihood, though that is one of his duties, but to lead his life as to [attain] . . . all of what is characteristic of, peculiar to, and highest in human nature; or, as the Greeks put it, to achieve the *aretē* of man.[5]

Excellence, "the instinct of the Greek race," motivated them to marvelous achievements in athletics, philosophy, architecture, art, science, literature, and many other fields. "When authentic excellence was seen in all of its radiant beauty, it became its own reward. Involvement in the process of attaining it became intensely gratifying."[6]

It is important to keep in mind that excellence describes God's very nature, a truth captured by the psalmist when he declared, "How excellent is thy name [i.e., nature] in all the earth" (Ps. 8:1, KJV). Interestingly, the Hebrew word for "glory" *(hod)* is translated *aretē* in the Septuagint (Hab. 3:3; Zech. 6:13). His glory is His excellence. The writer of Hebrews refers to the Son as "the radiance of God's glory and the exact representation of his being" (1:3).

If Jesus reflected God's glory by His excellent life and ministry, we who continue His work should do the same. That may seem impossible until you recall that it is "Christ in you, the hope of glory" (Col. 1:27). Moreover, Peter reminds us that "His divine power has granted to us everything pertaining to life and godliness, through the true knowledge of Him who called us by His own glory and excellence" (2 Pet. 1:3, NASB). The kind of excellence that glorifies God is characterized by *agapē,* love that cannot be manufactured but flows naturally from those who know Him. It is up to us to channel such love to the hurting around us, just as Jesus did. To the degree that this happens, we reflect the very nature and character of our excellent God.

Excellence is expensive; mediocrity is cheap. Admittedly, sometimes good is good enough because you can reach the point of diminishing returns on certain tasks. However, if you determine to strive for more than just getting by, it will really cost you in the currencies of time and energy. But the payoff is huge—in terms of personal gratification, the impact you have upon others, and, most importantly, the glory God receives.

With a very concerned expression on her face, a little lady spoke in condescending tones to D. L. Moody immediately after he had delivered a soul-stirring message. "Mr. Moody," she said solemnly, "you made thirty grammatical errors in the speech you just gave." "You are so very kind," he responded. "I'm sure there were more. There's one thing about it; I did my best." And then he bent over graciously and looking into her eyes asked, "My friend, are *you* doing *your* best?"

Key Concept: Balance

Immediately Jesus made the disciples get into the boat and go on ahead of him to the other side, while he dismissed the crowd. After he had dismissed them, he went up on a mountainside by himself to pray. When evening came, he was there alone, but the boat was already a considerable distance from land, buffeted by the waves because the wind was against it. During the fourth watch of the night Jesus went out to them, walking on the lake (Matt. 14:22-25).

Matthew's accounts of two dramatic nature miracles—Jesus' feeding of the 5,000 (vv. 13-21) and walking on the water (vv. 22-33)—sharpen His identity by emphasizing His unique power. Both have unmistakable messianic implications.

On the surface, the first episode simply looks like the supernatural satisfaction of a crowd's physical hunger on a specific occasion. It is much more. Keep in mind that the miracle described here involves the provision of food in "a remote place" (v. 15), reminiscent of manna in the wilderness. At a deeper level and in contrast to the feeding of the 4,000 (which points toward the Gentiles), this miracle with reference to the 12 baskets (which most likely symbolize the 12 tribes of Israel) is an indication that the Messiah has come to satisfy the Jews' spiritual hunger.

Matthew's next pericope reinforces the identity of Jesus as Messiah in an epiphany to the disciples akin to the Transfiguration. His fearful followers had been fighting the storm for a large part of the night when Jesus appeared before them walking on the lake. Given the popular belief that the sea was the home of evil spirits, the disciples undoubtedly believed that the "ghost" came to harm them. Not so. Jesus was there to calm the storm and the disciples' fear by clearly identifying himself. "Take courage! It is I. Don't be afraid" (v. 27). "It is I" is much more than a simple self-identification; in this theophany-like context, these words probably allude to the definition of Yahweh's name "I AM." As you know, in the aftermath of Peter's aborted wave-walking experience, the Master stilled the storm and those who were in the boat quickly acknowledged Him as the Son of God.

Sandwiched between these back-to-back narratives that confirm Jesus' identity is an instructive interlude (the printed passage above) that teaches us a vital lesson about His modus operandi. On the heels of the miraculous feeding, Jesus disengages from the crowd to be alone in prayer. There are several other references to Jesus praying in Matthew's Gospel (26:36, 39, 42, 44), all in connection with His imminent suffering and death. While such thoughts may have been on His mind during this occasion (perhaps prompted by the reports of John the Baptist's death), I believe that Jesus went to pray primarily out of a growing sense that He needed the batteries recharged.

He understood, better than anyone else, how ministry drains one physically, emotionally, and spiritually. So Jesus dismisses the needy crowd and temporarily separates himself from the ministry team to make His way up the mountainside. It is possible that the crowd and the Twelve were sent away in order to squelch any designs for a popular revolt; however, Matthew cites Jesus' desire to pray as the primary motivation for this withdrawal. The solitude of Jesus seems to be an important motif for Matthew, in light of the fact that he twice uses the Greek phrase that has been translated "privately" (14:13) and "by himself" and adds that "he was there alone" (v. 23). It's as if Matthew wants to make sure that we do not miss the point—Jesus' ministry was balanced between engaging and disengaging.

A careful reading of Matt. 14 reveals another reason for Jesus' mountainside retreat—the grieving of a loss. Verse 13 suggests that it was news of John the Baptist's beheading that originally prompted Jesus to withdraw to a solitary place. After all, John was His cousin and the two boys were born within six months of each other, in towns within sight of each other. The life of young John was hidden for nearly 30 years in the wilderness before he emerged to fulfill his life purpose as the forerunner of Jesus; however, it's probably safe to assume that the two boys knew each other and perhaps hung out together in their youth. No doubt, John's horrendous death would have triggered grief, and Jesus sought solitude on the sea in order to process it. There is no indication that He was fleeing from Herod Antipas; the loss of John led Jesus to get away for a while.

Friends often rally to support those who have lost family members to death, and rightfully so. Our visits, cards, flowers, and foods clearly communicate an important message: "We stand with you during these difficult days." Well-meaning counselors encourage mourners to stay busy and connected, as if solitude is the enemy of our souls. All that's OK—to a point. However, my experience in bereavement these past few years has taught me the valuable role of privacy in the grief process. The death of both parents within four months hit me like a ton of bricks. During several solo drives across America's dairyland, the Great Shepherd comforted and restored my soul.

Losses certainly are not limited to the passing of relatives; they include declining health and handicaps, geographical and/or emotional separation from children, fractured friendships, the death of dreams, and much, much more. Pastors are usually reluctant to lay aside the work long enough to properly grieve life's losses, but those who do will discover that solitude becomes a means of grace for us. Retreat occasionally—Jesus did. Of course, His grieving was temporarily interrupted by the needy who had followed the shoreline with their eyes on the Lord. Moved by compassion, Jesus engages the crowd—healing their sick and feeding the hungry. Engaging and disengaging. And the beat goes on.

No one captures the ebb and flow of our Lord's life as well as Luke. In a summary statement, he writes, "The news about [Jesus] spread all the more, so that crowds of people came to hear him and to be healed of their sicknesses. But Jesus often withdrew to lonely places and prayed" (Luke 5:15-16). The rebuke of the fever in Peter's mother-in-law created quite a stir in the community, leading the people to bring all their needy friends to Jesus for healing and exorcism. "At daybreak [the morning after the 'crusade'] Jesus went out to a solitary place" (4:42). Mark's narrative adds that when Simon and his companions found Jesus praying, "They exclaimed: 'Everyone is looking for you!'" (Mark 1:35).

When our Lord descended the mountain of Transfiguration with His inner circle (Peter, John, and James), "a large crowd met him" (Luke 9:37), and He immediately restored the health of a boy with an evil spirit (vv. 38-43). Engaging and disengaging. Near the end of His earthly journey, "each day Jesus was teaching at the temple, and each evening he went out to spend the night on the hill called the Mount of Olives, and all the people came early in the morning to hear him at the temple" (21:37-38). Jesus' mountaintop experiences prepared Him for the valley of need below. On at least one occasion, Jesus spent the entire night praying—apparently to discern the Father's will in connection with choosing the 12 apostles (6:12-13).

I have known a few pastors who were so disengaged that they could easily be mistaken for someone who is unemployed. If some of them got any slower, they'd be in reverse! They are downright lazy, but those who are intent on being politically correct would prefer to call them motivationally challenged.

Some of the disengaged are considered mystics. You know the hyperreflective types who are so heavenly-minded that they are of no earthly good. Like the inner circle of disciples, they often prefer building shelters in the glorified presence of Jesus and camping out there rather than descending into the valley of needs. For them, the perfect world is a nonstop spiritual formation retreat.

Most of us, however, do not like lonely places; we want to be where the action is—fully engaged. Like the Energizer Bunny, we keep going and going and going. There is nothing quite so exhilarating as our involvement with people whose lives are being radically transformed by the grace of God. It pumps us up! One victory leads to another as word spreads across bridges of friendship, and the spiritual renewal for which we have prayed becomes a reality. We can get so motivated by the moving of God's Spirit among us that if we're not careful to disengage occasionally, we run the risk of total burnout. Solitude is but a distant dream when "everyone is looking for you" and we start feeling indispensable. Even when we do make the occasional trip to the mountain, it is difficult to disengage from those who are "buffeted by the waves" (Matt. 14:24), because we struggle with feelings of false guilt. I have this mental image of the weary pastor praying with one eye open, surveying the situation below. We feel such responsibility for our people.

The Associated Press reported a "strange but true story" on July 8, 2005, involving 1,500 sheep that inexplicably jumped off the same cliff near the town of Gevas, Turkey, while their shepherds ate breakfast. At the end of the day, 450 dead animals lay on top of one another in a billowy white pile; a thousand or more were spared as the pile got higher and their fall was cushioned. The estimated loss to the 26 families who owned the wayward sheep tops $100,000.[7] As I read this bizarre story, my heart ached for those faithful, hardworking shepherds who may never enjoy unhurried moments at breakfast again. Our "sheep" can do some stupid things as well, adding to our concern for their anticipated needs. Is it just me or have you noticed that sheep always seem to be jumping over cliffs whenever we go to the mountain for "breakfast?" Lest we begin to feel as though we can never leave them unattended for a short while, let me remind you that we are responsible *to* them, not *for* them.

Disengagement is countercultural in a society where one's worth is usually measured in terms of doing, not being. America's transition from an industrial society to an information society is complete; nevertheless, hard work is still considered a virtue and no pastor wants to be called a slacker. We are praised and rewarded for overwork, despite the fact that it is one of Satan's weapons of mass destruction. Our parents and grandparents may have implied that *real work* is done with one's hands, not with the heart, soul, and mind. Such a utilitarian view is particularly problematic for us, since most pastoral work is intangible. Thus some pastors go to great lengths to prove that they are actually *doing* something and never stop to consider the harmful effects of overwork. We have been schooled to "find a need and fill it, find a hurt and heal it"; so we are tempted to descend the mountain prematurely and do what we can to help. Keep in mind that a renewed pastor, not a weary one, is better suited for effective ministry in the long run.

Remember this—if Jesus sensed a need to balance engaging and disengaging, doing and being, we better do the same. The life of Christ reveals the power of balance that emanates from spiritual renewal, insight into Scripture, a clearer picture of God's will, and a rested body. Some of you may be thinking, "I'd rather burn out than rust out!" Whether you burn out or rust out, you are still *out!* Those are not the only two options. Somewhere between workaholism and indolence, there is a balanced *Christian* approach that keeps us *in* the ministry—literally and emotionally.

Key Concept: Grace

Now the tax collectors and "sinners" were all gathering around to hear him. But the Pharisees and the teachers of the law muttered, "This man welcomes sinners and eats with them" (Luke 15:1-2).

There is probably no chapter in the New Testament so well known and so dearly loved as Luke 15—what some have called the gospel in the Gospel. Jesus shared three parables—the lost sheep, the lost coin, and the lost son—in response to the protest by the Pharisees and scribes related to the company He kept. Tax collectors were regarded as unclean on three counts: politically, because they were in the employment of the hated Roman occupation of Palestine; ceremonially, because their job brought them into constant contact with Gentiles; and morally, because they were almost always dishonest—guilty of extortion and exploitation by demanding more tax than they had any right to expect. It was an offense to these religious leaders that Jesus associated with men and women who, by the orthodox, were labeled sinners.

The Pharisees had a name for all those who did not keep the law—the People of the Land—and they went to great lengths to avoid interaction with "sinners." Pharisaic regulations were clear at this point: "When a man is one of the People of the Land, entrust no money to him, take no testimony from him, trust him with no secret, do not appoint him guardian of an orphan, do not make him the custodian of charitable funds, do not accompany him on a journey."[8] Jesus' practice of hanging out with the tax collectors and sinners was especially offensive, in light of the regulation that kept the Pharisees from socializing with the likes of them. Sharing meals with sinners, in particular, violated their specific rules for ritual cleanliness. Furthermore, a Pharisee was forbidden, as far as possible, to have business dealings with the People of the Land. The strict Jews did not say, "There is joy in heaven over one sinner who repents," but, "There is joy in heaven over one sinner who is obliterated before God."[9]

The Pharisees' exclusive behavior stands in sharp contrast to Jesus' gracious befriending of sinners—a behavior He defends and justifies by means of three classic parables. The Master Teacher challenges them to recognize that were the loss their own, their behavior would be the same as that described in each parable. Though the man described in the first parable has 99 other sheep, it is quite natural for him to give a disproportionate amount of time and attention to the one that is lost. You see the same line of thinking in the parable of the lost coin and the lost son. The thrust is clear: lost people matter to God and they should matter to us. The motif of shared joy in each of the stories implies that the church should continue to befriend sinners and rejoice together when one is saved.

"This man welcomes sinners and eats with them," muttered the Pharisees and teachers of the Law. Some of Jesus' greatest compliments came unintentionally from His critics, and this is certainly one of them. What a commendation. It's a succinct summary of God's amazing grace, channeled through His Son. If Jesus is to become our pastoral model, this statement holds profound implications for the focus of our ministry.

It is often said that you can tell what a person is like by the company he or she keeps. There is a measure of truth in that. Yes, birds of a feather flock together. However, I submit that you must consider the motives of people in regard to the company they keep. Why does he or she choose to associate with a particular person? It is possible to seek someone's company not because you approve of the person's lifestyle but because you hope to have some influence in changing him or her. Teachers hang out with kids with an eye toward educating them. Doctors spend time with the sick in hopes of restoring their health—the very point Jesus made in response to the Pharisees' consternation about His dinner party with Levi and his tax-collector colleagues. "It is not the healthy who need a doctor," Jesus said, "but the sick. I have not come to call the righteous, but sinners" (Mark 2:17). It never occurred to the Pharisees that Jesus might have kept bad company for a good reason. He did and so should we.

Unfortunately, many church leaders adopt an "us vs. them" attitude and proceed to build walls (like the Pharisees) instead of bridges (like Jesus). I read somewhere that such a dichotomous worldview may have its roots in our underlying anger toward those sinners who have messed up our "Christian nation" with their wicked ways. It is arguable whether or not we have ever been a truly Christian nation; nevertheless, one could never justify selfish anger toward the unrighteous, even if some of our country's woes can be linked to them. Our subconscious anger may explain, at least in part, why befriending love for sinners is so rare. It's difficult to act in loving ways toward those with whom you are angry. Ambivalent feelings paralyze us. I suspect that the spirit of the Pharisee lurks near each of our hearts.

Your distance from sinners could be traced to a much nobler cause—the quantity and quality of your work rendered within church structures. "After all," we reason, "they pay me to do a job." Keep in mind, however, that you work for God—not the church; the church provides your livelihood, not your marching orders. It's not as though anyone intentionally sets out to ignore sinners; we simply become preoccupied with the members and invest far too much of our time and energy into the holy huddle. Let's face it—"there is in the Church such hallowed fellowship as cannot otherwise be known"; it just seems so natural and right to associate with believers. I have always felt that one could partially gauge the health of a church by its fellowship factor—that is, how long the members linger in the foyer following a worship service.

We really enjoy each other's company. However, we must bear in mind that there are countless others who need our holy hugs. The Church possesses what someone has called an ambidextrous calling—on the one hand, we are to be in the world; on the other hand, we are not to be of the world. It would appear, however, that we have taken the doctrine of separation too far, perhaps fearing contamination by sinners, and insulated ourselves from them. Preoccupied with oiling the ecclesiastical machinery and attending to the concerns of the healthy, we have been guilty of ignoring those who are desperately ill just beyond our doors.

Graciously befriending sinners is countercultural on two fronts. First, most of our churches are inwardly focused sanctuaries for those who are content with business as usual and taking care of our own. We exegete the Great Commission better than we execute it. Most discussions about ministry opportunities focus on filling church positions and seldom include befriending sinners outside the church; in some cases, pastors even withhold their blessing on beyond-the-walls ministry because it diverts energy from church programs. Upon reading most church bulletins and newsletters, I am left with the distinct impression that we have mistaken activity for ministry—especially in the so-called seven days a week churches where weekly programs range from the study of biblical languages to aerobics and quilting. Sadly, we seem to be obsessed with running programs that any secular organization could provide. Let's remember that what makes the Church the Church is its *Christian* mission—befriending sinners, loving them into the Kingdom, and making disciples out of believers. Expect such *Christian* ministry to upset the Pharisees among us because attention given to sinners could be directed toward their needs, and besides, we've never done it that way before!

Second, befriending sinners is contrary to the impersonal spirit of this age. Unfortunately, there seems to be an unwritten rule passed along from generation to generation that suggests that respectable people do not hang out with "those kinds of people." Fear, prejudice, and pride are prompting many to embrace an exclusive lifestyle evidenced by the increase in gated communities, private clubs, private schools, and so on. Neighbors hardly know one another. Cyber-friendships are popular with the younger generation; teens may have as many on-line friends around the world as they have at school. Reports of terrorism, violence, and abuse have made us more and more suspicious of strangers. We look beyond each other in crowds.

Pastor friends, we must lead the way if our people are going to catch the vision of befriending sinners. Practice what you preach. Just say no to the frivolous demands upon your time and energy, so that you can make heart connections with sinners who may never darken the doors of your church. Someone said, "The church is the only institution which exists for its nonmembers." Most of us would agree with that, but mental assent must be translated into action at this point, if we are following Jesus' example.

Key Concept: Accountability

From everyone who has been given much, much will be demanded; and from the one who has been entrusted with much, much more will be asked (Luke 12:48).

Watchfulness may be the term that best describes Luke 12:35-48, a collection of brief parables and attached sayings. The challenge is clear: be ready for the coming judgment. When waiting for their master's return from a wedding banquet, the servants are advised to stay dressed in a manner fitting immediate presentation before the master and to keep their lamps burning so they can open the door for him immediately. "The typical long robe of ancient dress was worn loose when one was at leisure in private but tied in place whenever one needed to be 'dressed for the occasion' or to be active in work, travel, or warfare."[10] The watchful, according to the parable, will be rewarded with a role reversal—the master will become their servant (vv. 35-38).

Luke advances the watchfulness theme by adding Jesus' story of the thief breaking into one's house unannounced (v. 39). The lesson is self-evident. If one doesn't want to be surprised by the Lord's return, he or she should always be ready.

Peter then questions the Lord about His intended audience: "Are you telling this parable to us [the disciples], or to everyone?" (v. 41). Jesus responds with a question of His own ("Who then is the faithful and wise manager?" [v. 42]) and proceeds to answer it by stating the reward for those who are found faithful and the severe punishment for the slothful, wicked servant. In the end, the answer to Peter's question becomes crystal clear in the words of the printed passage above. The bottom line is this: while everyone is accountable to the Master, the privileged servant who has been entrusted with a special task (the disciples and us) is more answerable to the degree that we are more aware of His will. We, like the disciples, have been "entrusted with much." Therefore, "much, much more will be asked" (v. 48). Opportunity and responsibility are inseparable.

In the final analysis, Jesus has issued a call to stewardship accountability—in light of a day of reckoning, the final judgment with its rewards and punishments. Those who take His Word seriously will "be dressed ready for service" and faithfully perform our duties until the Master returns and/or calls us home. Maximizing pastors are not satisfied while work remains undone or half done; instead, they anticipate a day when they can echo the words of Jesus: "I have brought you glory on earth by completing the work you gave me to do" (John 17:4).

Jesus clearly taught that a day of judgment is coming when every person will be called upon to give an account of his or her life. For instance, in a context where the Pharisees had spoken evil of Jesus by attributing His miracles to Satan, Jesus made the point that people are responsible for all their actions and words that will acquit or condemn them on the day of judgment. He said, "Men will have to give account on the day of judgment for every careless word they have spoken" (Matt. 12:36).

With the prospect of ultimate accountability looming on the horizon, you would think that all of us would bring our A game to the pastoral assignment on a daily basis. Not so. Careless conduct is commonplace in our ranks. I don't want to be guilty of painting with too broad of a brush here, but it appears to me that some pastors come dangerously close to resembling the slothful servant. They may not be getting drunk or beating the menservants and maidservants, but their irresponsibility suggests that accountability to God is the last thing on their minds. Friends, we only go around once in life—no mulligans, no do-overs. Your present life is not a dress rehearsal for another one. Let's be more diligent about girding our robes and attending to the Master's business so we will be found faithful when the last trumpet sounds.

Perhaps this is another point at which we are being squeezed into society's mold. During the past few decades, this country has experienced a monumental shift from a God-centered perspective to a human-centered perspective, resulting in a very individualistic culture (as noted earlier). As you would know, the trend these days is for humans to make God accountable to them for their comfort and pleasure, not vice versa. The prevailing attitude is that a person is responsible to no one but himself or herself. For most Americans, the term *accountability* conjures up images of heavy-handed coercion, invasion of privacy, and manipulative practices. What's worse is that we have become "a nation of victims" (to employ Charles Sykes' term) whose mantra is, "I am not responsible; it's not my fault." These days, people are more concerned with justifying their behavior than owning up to responsibility. Personal accountability gets lost in a sea of excuses, such as bad parents, racism, sexism, illness, and addiction.

Our text implies that accountability is one of the means God uses to bring out the best in us. Please note, however, that His plan involves lines of responsibility that run vertically *and horizontally.* Knowing that we are sheep who are prone to wander, God invites us to enter accountable relationships with fellow sojourners for the purpose of holding us accountable to Him—a recurring theme throughout the New Testament, pronounced in Paul's "one another" passages. The apostle's own connections with Timothy, Titus, Barnabas, and others confirm the priority he placed on horizontal accountability.

For the first couple of years in my current assignment, I didn't know enough about the district superintendency to know how much I didn't know. My ministry was more *reactive* than *proactive.* I am now convinced that the greatest contribution a judicatory leader can make in the advancement of the Kingdom involves nudging the ministry team members toward optimal ministry with equal doses of encouragement and accountability. When those of us who are responsible for demanding the best from pastors grant exceptions, we become accomplices in halfhearted efforts and sanction mediocrity. Mutual accountability is vital to maximum performance.

Authenticity, servanthood, obedience, excellence, balance, grace, and accountability—these are the foundational pillars upon which a solid *Christian* ministry is built. There may be more, but common sense compels me to move now from the abstract to the concrete. Some pastoral theology books leave me longing for more practical application. Frankly, authors who leave it up to the reader to connect the dots frustrate me. I hope to do better, at the risk of insulting your intelligence. How does one translate these Christian ministry *principles* into pastoral *practices*? I intend to address that all-important question by offering a ministry model that takes into account the *whole person.*

A BALANCED MINISTRY MODEL FOR MAXIMIZING PASTORS

Maximizing Pastors Are Spiritually Aligned

While there is no particular priority implied in the listing of the 15 factors of chapter 2 and the six key concepts just discussed, I have purposely placed spiritual alignment with the Lord in the lead-off position here because we can do absolutely nothing of eternal value apart from Him. The corollary is also true—we "can do all things through Him who strengthens" us (Phil. 4:13, NASB). As pastors, we are engaged in a supernatural ministry and must not attempt to do this work in our natural power. It's a mission impossible. That's why P. T. Forsyth said, "You must live with people to know their problems, and live with God in order to solve them."[11]

That is easier said than done, considering the frenetic pace of our lives. Fred Silva, a Brazilian theologian, makes this sobering observation: "I am not convinced North Americans, particularly North American men, can have an intimate relationship with God. You don't do relationships well. Your whole society is based on completing projects."[12] Fred is right. We are guilty as charged, and our obsession with doing is crippling our ministries.

At a fairly recent denominational gathering, guest speaker Dr. Dennis Kinlaw likened the holy life to the intimacy of marriage and dared to ask us the $64,000 question: "Does your ministry flow out of your relationship with Jesus or does your relationship with Jesus come from your ministry?" A holy hush came over the assembly. Conviction came. I humbly acknowledged before God my propensity to favor doing over being and sought forgiveness for temporarily neglecting soul-care. Kinlaw's question has echoed in the corridors of my mind ever since that meeting; it's a gentle reminder that spiritual alignment is fundamental to our professional growth.

Spiritual alignment requires both *me-time* and *we-time*. In the contemporary vernacular, *me-time* refers to a period when someone relaxes by doing something that he or she enjoys—getting a massage or a pedicure, going for a drive, and so on. The idea is that amid the stress of 21st-century life and the nonstop demands of work and family, it is increasingly more difficult to spend time that is exclusively devoted to one's own revitalization.

Maximizing pastors embrace the idea that self-preservation is not self-indulgent and make me-time a regular part of the daily routine. I have in mind the me-time that honors the wisdom of Prov. 4:23: "Watch over your heart with all diligence, for from it flow the springs of life" (NASB). If *me-time* sounds too selfish for you, feel free to revert to the more traditional labels such as *devotional* or *quiet time*. I favor the emerging term because spending time with Jesus is both *enjoyable* and *restorative*, thus qualifying as me-time by definition. And wonder of wonders—Jesus enjoys our company too! Others are shouting for our attention; He whispers, "Come to me, all you who are weary and burdened, and I will give you rest. Take my yoke upon you and learn from me, for I am gentle and humble in heart, and you will find rest for your souls" (Matt. 11:28-29). That's music to the ears of pastors who know that "the load of tomorrow, added to that of yesterday, carried today makes the strongest falter."[13]

Those who are serious about spiritual alignment will consider me-time a joyful delight, not a dreary duty. They may be overheard saying, "I *get to* spend time with Jesus" instead of, "I've *got to* do devotions." Seventy-one percent of the maximizing pastors responding to my survey have accepted the Lord's gracious invitation and meet with Him at a specific time and place each day; 79 percent read the Bible devotionally each day; 38 percent practice spiritual journaling.

A word of warning is in order at this point. If pastors are not extremely careful, they will allow communication, not communion, to become the primary motivation for Scripture reading. Feed your sheep, my friend, but feed yourself as well. The Bible is much more than the happy hunting ground for Sunday's sermons; it is God's love letter to His children. Read it devotionally, not homiletically, during me-time.

All this talk about me-time with Jesus may seem unnecessary, given my target audience—preachers. I can imagine that some may simply dismiss it as preaching to the choir. Not so fast. One of our occupational hazards is being lulled into thinking that talking *about* God takes the place of talking *with* God. Nothing could be further from the truth. The idea must have originated with the father of lies who, no doubt, would be pleased for us to speak vociferously for a God we hardly know. Prayer is the chief agency whereby we enhance and monitor our personal relationship with Jesus Christ; it's also the means for aligning ourselves with His purposes. Therefore, we should be careful not to pester God for personal benefits or His blessing upon *our* plans instead of listening for His.

One day a friend of Phillips Brooks, the legendary preacher of another generation, called on him and found him impatiently pacing the floor. He asked what the trouble was. With flashing eyes Dr. Brooks exclaimed, "The trouble is that I am in a hurry and God is not!"[14] For that reason, I recommend quarterly, semiannual, or annual spiritual formation retreats that remove us from the urgent demands of the workaday world to unhurried hours at the feet of Jesus. Most of us leave the mountain of prayer too early because we are in a rush and do not want to give the impression that we are shirking responsibilities. But those who wait on the Lord renew their strength (Isa. 40:31), reduce their worry, and receive their marching orders.

We-time supplements our me-time for spiritual alignment. I define we-time as moments spent in an affirmation/accountability relationship with trusted Christian friends. Howard Hendricks said, "Every man should have three individuals in his life: a Paul, a Barnabas, and a Timothy."[15] This principle is applicable to both men and women; however, for the sake of maintaining moral purity, these individuals should be of the same sex. Hendricks describes a Paul as an older man who is willing to mentor you; someone who has been down the road before you and wants to share what he has learned in the laboratory of life. A Barnabas is a soul brother, someone who loves you but is willing to keep you honest and accountable. A Timothy is a younger man into whom you are pouring your life and wisdom. My life has been blessed and enriched by several in each of these categories.

By the way, 53 percent of the maximizing pastors surveyed meet with someone for spiritual accountability on a regular basis. Is there someone in your life who affirms but cares enough to confront you with the tough questions about spiritual life and leadership? There should be.

Choose your we-time partners prayerfully. Establish your relationship roles clearly. Meet with them regularly. Begin and end your sessions promptly. Share your life openly. Accept their counsel humbly.

It is God's intention to reproduce His likeness in us, making us spiritual leaders in the truest sense of the word. At the end of the day, pastors who will be led more *by* Jesus lead more *like* Jesus and lead more *to* Jesus.

Maximizing Pastors Are Emotionally Connected

There is no silver bullet when it comes to maximizing one's potential. However, if pressed to identify the one thing that would most likely transform a good minister into a great one, I would cite improvement in the quality of interpersonal relationships.

Without a doubt, our families top the list. Stay emotionally connected to the most important members of the congregation—your spouse and children. They are God's most precious gifts to you. Do not take them for granted; strengthen the ties that bind you together. You know it is possible to be emotionally absent even when you are physically present. Spend quality time with each member of your family on a regular basis—making sure you remain in the moment instead of entertaining distracting thoughts about pressing issues. Let your spouse and kids be themselves, not what church members expect them to be. If you insist on making a family member the subject of a sermon illustration, be sure you portray him or her in a positive light.

When asked about priority relationships, most of us tend to place

God, family, church, and others in a simple column. The inference is that family always takes precedence over the church, and frankly, it is hard to dispute that point. However, a static listing fails to take account that sometimes what the family wants us to do may not square with what God desires. For instance, your daughter may have 30 soccer games during the course of a season, and a static listing of priorities calls for your attendance at every one of them—even when it means ignoring *kairos* (God's timing) for a conversation with someone seeking to find Him. I prefer a more dynamic view of priorities captured in the simple illustration below.

Priority Relationships

In this model, the Christ-centered person realizes that all the priority relationships with others are subject to varying levels of attention depending upon changing life circumstances. Admittedly, there may be moments when we feel conflicted over competing priorities, but usually there is a clear sense of divine ought. An inner assurance that we are doing what God wants us to do then and there allows us to be fully engaged in the moment without suffering from false guilt. Call me naive, if you must; nonetheless, I accept the wisdom of Prov. 3:6: "In all thy ways acknowledge him, and he shall direct thy paths" (KJV).

The pastor-priest role is all about connecting people with God; however, we cannot do that effectively from a distance. Many people in the helping occupations prefer to remain rather aloof from those they serve, relating to them professionally but not personally. Doctors, counselors, and social workers immediately come to mind. I suspect that it's a defense mechanism to avoid compassion fatigue and the inevitable disappointments associated with the people business. But as pastors, the effectiveness of our dealings with people, in large measure, hinges upon our willingness to come alongside and emotionally engage them. Whatever concerns them concerns us. And the adage is true: "They don't care how much we know until they know how much we care!" Like it or not, we are in the people business, so it's not a matter of *whether* we are going to relate to them but *how*. I contend that getting *along* with people is fundamental to working with them, but getting *close* is necessary for working well together. In my opinion, making heart connections must occupy a prominent place on our list of priorities.

Personal warmth comes naturally to some of us. I happen to be one of those who gets juiced up by company and conversation; my wife would tell you I have mastered the art of table-hopping during banquets. Nonetheless, there are some pastors who prefer to read bulletin boards before and after worship services instead of engaging their church members. The introverts will need to move out of their comfort zone and become more intentional about connecting with people in order to be all they can be.

If you need convincing at this point, consider the following benefits of healthy human relationships:

- Care for the souls of your parishioners will improve your preaching and teaching. The true prophet identifies with the community within which he or she speaks, and that connection enables the prophet to better relate the ancient Word to contemporary issues. Our best preaching emerges from community life, not a vacuum. Moreover, people are more teachable when they possess warm feelings about the teacher/preacher. If you preach a sermon that is a solid 7 on a scale of 1 to 10, people with whom you have relationally connected will hear it as a 9. The opposite is also true. That same sermon may be considered a 5 by those who do not know you well or simply don't like you.

- People gladly follow the leadership of those they know and trust. In *The Seven Habits of Highly Effective People,* Stephen Covey encourages leaders to consider their dealings with others in terms of an emotional bank account—a metaphor that describes the amount of trust that's been built up in a relationship. We make deposits to the account by understanding the individual, attending to the little things, keeping commitments, clarifying expectations, showing personal integrity, and apologizing sincerely when we make a withdrawal from the account.[16] As a result, people become more receptive to our spiritual direction in their lives.

- Close connections with people enable us to recognize a problem before it becomes an emergency. Like Smokey the Bear, engaging pastors will sniff the air and "find a fire before it starts to flame."

- Healthy pastor-parishioner relationships provide insight into what motivates our church members, enabling us to customize our appeals to a particular individual. The key motivational indicators will never be discovered via surface relationships.

- Strong ties with your people create a climate for change. Whenever a trusted pastor makes an out of the boat proposal, he or she has a small army of early adopters who will probably help sell it to other members of the congregation all the way to the point of critical mass. It's difficult to lead a congregation through major changes; it's impossible without warm fuzzies between the pastor and his or her people.

- Engaging pastors encourage shared thinking that yields better decisions.

- If there's a strong marriage between pastor and people, church members are likely to overlook the pastor's blunders. Love is blind.

- Loving links between the shepherd and the sheep enhance the congregation's outreach efforts because humans are bonding beings who long for intimacy. People go to the church nearest their heart, not nearest their home!

- Finally, up close and personal relationships allow the pastor to model holiness through the mountaintops and valleys of life. An ounce of example is worth a pound of preach.

Will pastoral care become another casualty of our society's urbanization, modernization, and secularization? I hope not. Admittedly, we are struggling to redefine pastoral care in the wake of major sociological shifts: the rising number of women in the workplace, the mobility of modern life, technological advances that keep families connected to each other and to cyber-friends on several continents, longer work days (made longer by commutes), the cocooning mind-set, an increasing number of recreational options and discretionary funds that make them accessible. And yet, in this topsy-turvy world, basic human needs remain the same and the pastor is still God's primary agent for centering people in Christ.

Some have spurned the traditional pastoral call; only a few have come up with effective alternatives. Is there still a place for home visits in 21st-century America? I think so. In fact, I would argue it is the very conditions that make pastoral calling *difficult* that make it so *important.* Keep in mind that many of your people are constantly on the go to ease the pain of an empty life. In Thoreau's day, the masses may have been leading lives of quiet desperation; these days, most are filling their lives with quirky distractions. If that's true, we pastors are responsible to call on our overscheduled friends and invite them back to "the peace that Jesus gives." It is a real challenge to connect with fast-forwarding folk who may or may not be receptive to your visit. There's wisdom in making an appointment, in most cases. Prayerfully plan your visit with a redemptive aim in mind. Arrive promptly, briefly exchange pleasantries, ask about their spiritual journey, listen carefully, affirm when possible, offer counsel when appropriate, read Scripture, and pray. By all means, do not overstay your welcome. Maybe it's just wishful thinking on my part, but I still believe that most church members appreciate a home visit with a distinctively pastoral purpose.

However, I believe that some of our best pastoral care is rendered on the go when it is least expected—often in social situations. Your church members are more likely to open up to you in the relaxed atmosphere surrounding a dinner, ball game, or party; the discerning shepherd will listen for their words and the pain behind them. Obviously, some social settings are not conducive to prolonged conversation; however, there's almost always enough time for an encouraging word, a scriptural promise, and/or a brief prayer offered on their behalf. If you wait for the perfect environment (whatever that is) to engage in spiritual dialogue, you may miss the chance of a lifetime in a lifetime of chance.

There is no substitute for high-touch in a high-tech world; however, technology is the shepherd's friend in the never-ending effort to provide spiritual care. PCs allow you to connect with people around the block or around the globe, giving new meaning to Wesley's statement, "The world is my parish." These days we can offer real-time ministry to the multitudes via e-mail, e-cards, church Web sites, blogging, video conferencing, and so on. The cell phone may redeem our windshield time, if we are comfortable enough with multitasking to call our parishioners while driving. One pastor friend calls every member of his congregation on his or her birthday just to say, "I love and appreciate you." It takes just a few seconds but makes a lasting impression. Go ahead— embrace technology; the devil doesn't own the franchise on these tools.

The nurture of souls is not the exclusive domain of professionals. Convinced that God has entrusted the necessary gifts to the Body, the maximizing pastor abandons the sole caregiver mentality in favor of the *congregational care model.* It's both biblical and practical (see John 21:15-17; Acts 6:1-7). Let's face it—no one person, regardless of his or her energy level or giftedness, is able to provide adequate spiritual nurture for all members of the flock. However, we can enlist, train, and empower lay undershepherds for this vital ministry that, in some circles, has been off limits to them in the past.

If you are resistant to this idea, pause for a moment and ask yourself why. Could it be that your need to be needed has kept you from delegation at this point? Are you feeling pressed for time (like the Egyptian mummy) and unable to fit the necessary lay training into your busy schedule? Or maybe you simply are not convinced that pastoral work can and should be shared with the laity? Those who choose to be the sole caregivers in a congregation, for whatever reason, are limiting their influence and robbing others of meaningful ministry opportunities. I believe that congregational care is what the apostle Paul had in mind when he called on the Corinthians to "comfort those in any trouble with the comfort we ourselves have received from God" (2 Cor. 1:4).

Such care is better caught than taught. If you set out to create a nurturing climate in the church, you must model it consistently by attending to the little things. The little things are big things in human relationships. Those big little things include knowing everyone's name (including the children), remembering special occasions, listening carefully to their concerns, offering hope, catching people doing something right, offering third-person compliments, and treating others as you would want to be treated (Matt. 7:12; Luke 6:31). Long after our parishioners have forgotten our very best sermons, they will remember how well we lived before them.

The unchurched will also take note of how we live, especially if we are emotionally connected to them. My hunch, however, is that most of us are fairly isolated from sinners. I am. In recent days, however, God has been nudging me out of the safety and security of the holy huddle into a position where He can use me as salt and light. Not long ago, my wife and I both faced the grave realization that neither of us had unchurched friends. Acquaintances? Sure. Friends? Not really. She planned a Christmas open house for our neighbors and began volunteer work at a local hospital; I took a part-time job as a starter at a nearby golf course. OK, I had a secondary motive as well—free golf! While none of our new friends have accepted Christ yet, our emotional connections are strong and bode well for spiritual victories down the road.

None of us will ever forget the compelling images of Hurricane Katrina victims on the rooftops of their flooded homes and hotels desperately seeking help. They scrawled SOS messages on bedsheets or whatever they could get their hands on and frantically waved to rescuers in Coast Guard helicopters. Thousands were airlifted to safety. Within your web of influence *(oikos)*, there are countless individuals reeling from sin's devastation upon their lives. Their cries for help are more subtle and could go unnoticed from a distance. Draw close to them and make them your friends, not your project.

Finally, the maximizing pastor connects with colleagues—friends both inside and outside his or her denominational family—who can identify with the ups and downs of the pastoral roller coaster ride. We need them as prayer partners, soul and role mentors, sounding boards, and friends with whom we can just let our hair down.

From the beginning, Christian leadership has been collegial—not competitive. As you may recall, Kenneth Christian's list of under-achieving types included rebels who resist authority and are suspicious of what they feel are others' attempts to exploit or control them. Pastoral rebels often find excuses to avoid denominational meetings such as district conventions, team-training events, and retreats. Sound familiar? If you are a rebel, search your heart for the reason why you have pulled away from the district ministry team; apologize, if it's appropriate; prayerfully consider an attitude adjustment; consider the upside of hanging out with your colleagues; reconnect and share your journey with those who can identify with your situation. Movement in that direction will result in personal satisfaction and professional growth. And who knows—you just may be pleasantly surprised by the affirmation received among your peers.

Whenever you are tempted to put down someone else's ministry to bolster your own, remember how Paul addressed the divisions within the Corinthian church that were apparently rooted in preacher worship. Paul identified Apollos as a partner in ministry who watered the seed he had planted. Both were mere men, but many came to faith through them because they worked in tandem (see 1 Cor. 3:1-9).

Hands play a major role in ordination services. Usually the presiding church official firmly places both hands atop the head of the ordinand and proclaims something to the effect, "I charge thee before God and the Lord Jesus Christ, preach the Word, watch thou in all things, endure afflictions, do the work of an evangelist, make full proof of thy ministry. Take thou authority to administer the sacraments and take oversight of the church of God. And now, by the authority vested in me . . . I ordain thee an elder in the church of God in the name of the Father, Son, and Holy Spirit, Amen."[17] Those pressing palms represent the huge responsibility associated with vocational ministry. Furthermore, in some churches elders lay their hands on the candidate during the ritual and shake his or her hand afterward. The imagery is telling. Although pastoral work can be burdensome, we are strengthened by the ongoing support of our colleagues. While peer learning enhances our competencies, it may be the knowledge that we are not in this battle alone that keeps us on the front lines of ministry. That's why it is so important to keep close to our ministerial brothers and sisters.

To my knowledge, the following quotation attributed to Dag Hammarskjöld, past secretary-general of the United Nations, was not directed toward pastors but is certainly applicable to this discussion: "It is more noble to give yourself completely to one individual than to labor diligently for the salvation of the masses."[18] I take that to mean that heart connections with others are much more important than surface relationships.

We all know that it's quite possible to be there with someone without *being there*. Given the *breadth* of a pastor's relationships, what can a person do to ensure their *depth*? The short answer is to grow forward in our relational competencies that include self-confidence, self-control, social skills, empathy, patience, openness, trust, and enjoyment. For example, the pastor who lacks empathy but wants to engage people on a deeper level could and should develop a growth plan that stretches him or her to practice listening skills such as temporarily squelching one's opinion; asking clarifying questions; summarizing what he or she thought he or she heard; and respectfully acknowledging a different point of view using phrases like, "I think I understand what you are saying" or "I can see why that makes sense." Another pastor may struggle with transparency. His or her plan would include a commitment to join a small group where openness is practiced in the strictest confidence. The pastor who needs to put the fun back in the fundamentals of pastoral ministry should devise a scheme that requires him or her to fully disconnect occasionally and regularly do some things for the sheer joy they bring. Growth in these competencies deepens our interpersonal relationships, restores positive emotion, and fuels high performance.

The maximizing pastor makes an intentional effort to be closely linked with family, church members, nonbelievers, and colleagues. In the context of authentic relationships on these various fronts, the love of God becomes visible.

Maximizing Pastors Are Physically Energized

Physical energy is vital to the performance of an athlete, soldier, or dancer. But because pastoral evaluations tend to focus more on what we do with our minds than with our bodies, we often overlook the significant role that physical energy plays in our lives. It is our fundamental source of fuel.

Are you tired of being tired? It is incumbent upon the would-be maximizing pastor to explore the question of how to keep one's energy reservoir replenished. You may be well acquainted with some of the ideas advanced in this section because of society's obsession with the latest health and fitness trends. The lack of accurate information doesn't seem to be a major problem; most of us simply need to do what we already know to do. So let us review the fitness basics—breathing, eating, sleeping, exercising, and laughing. A rhythmic balance between the expenditure of physical energy and recovery ensures that we have enough fuel in the tank to carry on; pushing past our comfort zone is the means by which we expand our physical capacity for peak performance.

We may take for granted one of the most important rhythms of life —our breathing. Most of us do not give it a second thought. We should. Here's why. Breathing is a simple, yet powerful, tool—a means both to summon energy and to relax deeply. Extended exhalations are particularly refreshing. It's no secret that anxiety and anger prompt faster and shallower breathing. What you may not know is that such a breathing pattern reduces our energy and ability to restore mental/emotional balance. Take deep abdominal breaths in stressful situations; they make keep you from a stupid, shoot-from-the-hip reaction.

Foods are another critical source of physical energy. Although most of us have never experienced *real* hunger, we are aware that the lack of food impairs a person's ability to function effectively. It's easy for us to forget that chronic overeating, which leads to obesity and a lack of energy, has the same effect. Nutritionists tell us that foods high in fats, sugar, and simple carbohydrates provide energy recovery, albeit in a much less energy-rich form than low-fat proteins and complex carbohydrates such as vegetables and grains. Eating well has obvious benefits —improving health, better looks, increased self-confidence, and more energy—all of which bode well for maximum performance.

Breakfast is the most important meal of the day; it increases blood glucose levels and jump-starts your metabolism in the morning. Experts recommend foods that are low on the glycemic index (which measures the speed at which sugar from specific foods is released into the bloodstream) and provide the longest lasting source of energy, such as whole grains, proteins, and fruits (strawberries, pears, grapefruit, and apples). Avoid high-glycemic foods such as muffins or sugared cereals; they prompt an energy spike that leads to a quick crash. It may surprise you to learn that a seemingly healthy breakfast consisting of a plain bagel and orange juice is very high on the glycemic index and thus a poor source for sustaining energy. Five to six low-calorie, highly nutritious meals at regular intervals each day provide a steady supply of vitality. Of course, portion control is critical—no supersizing. Since energy requirements diminish and the metabolism slows as evening approaches, eat more calories earlier in the day than you do when the sun goes down.[19]

A growing body of research makes water the most attractive drink option. Water is an inexpensive source of energy with health and longevity benefits. Caffeinated drinks such as coffee, tea, and diet colas provide temporary surges of energy that are not sustained throughout the course of a day and may keep you awake at night.

Adequate sleep is absolutely necessary for peak performance. I will not camp here too long, since the subject was briefly addressed in the section on neglect of the temple. Suffice it to say that the average human being needs seven to nine hours of sleep per night to maintain high levels of physical energy and to function optimally. Interestingly, numerous studies suggest that the specific times we sleep also affect our energy levels. For example, shift workers (those who sleep during the day) have twice the number of highway accidents as day workers and more job-related accidents as well.[20]

Our energy ebbs and flows in natural rhythms throughout the course of a day, reaching its lowest point around 3 or 4 P.M. This explains why many cultures intuitively normalized the midafternoon nap. It might be wise for each of us to adopt the practice. "NASA's Fatigue Counter Measures Program has found that a short nap of just forty minutes improved performance by an average of 34 percent and alertness by 100 percent."[21] Pastors who find ways to take brief recovery breaks during the course of a day are more likely to sustain a high energy level well into the evening.

I should hasten to add that strength and cardiovascular exercises also increase our energy levels, enhance our performance, and lift our spirits. The maximizing pastor will push past his or her comfort zone in a regimen that may include sprinting, walking/running on a treadmill, climbing steps, bicycling, weight lifting, swimming, or any number of other options—so long as the effect is to raise and lower heart rate. The key to any successful exercise program is to start slowly, build incrementally, and proceed consistently.

Finally, do not underestimate the power of laughter to energize us. There is a growing body of research evidence supporting the familiar claim that laughter is the best medicine. It decreases stress hormones, improves our immune system, and boosts endorphins (feel-good hormones). Lighten up. Don't take yourself too seriously. Laugh often. Even if you are faking it, you will get the same healthy benefits. While there are 5,000 laughter clubs in 50 countries around the world, pastors do not need to join any of them because the funniest things happen in and around the church.

Maximizing Pastors Are Mentally Focused

To perform at their best, pastors must be able to sustain concentration on the tasks at hand while holding fast to realistic optimism—a paradoxical notion that implies seeing the world as it is and partnering with

God to improve conditions, as His kingdom comes. Concentration requires physical energy, so we must balance expending and recovering it.

In most work environments, including the church, people believe that working longer hours is the best route to higher productivity. With few exceptions in cutting-edge businesses, employees are not rewarded for taking regular breaks or scheduling a workout. Thinking drains our energy. Thus those who are intent on maximizing their potential need to give the thinking mind its intermittent rest.

Where are you when you get your best ideas? That's the question posed by Michael Gelb in his insightful book titled *How to Think Like Leonardo da Vinci*. Thousands have provided him answers across the years and the most common are: "in the shower," "resting in bed," "walking in nature," and "listening to music." Gelb notes that "almost no one claims to get their best ideas at work." You will recall that Leonardo da Vinci was a prolific artist, and yet he hit the pause button several times each day—often taking a short nap. During his work on *The Lord's Supper*, da Vinci intentionally laid down his brush for regular breaks, much to the chagrin of his employer—the prior of Santa Maria delle Grazie. In response to his "pick up the pace" requests, da Vinci replied, "The greatest geniuses sometimes accomplish more when they work less."[22]

Experts agree that the creative process is oscillatory, engaging both hemispheres of the brain. The name Roger Sperry may not mean anything to you, but most of us are familiar with the neurosurgeon's Nobel Prize winning research establishing two fundamentally different ways of processing information. The left brain is the seat of language and operates in a rather analytical, logical manner; the right brain is more inclined to solve problems by intuition and sudden insight. Sperry's groundbreaking research explains why our best ideas often come to us when we least expect them—when we are far away from the office. Slacking is counterintuitive to the maximizing pastor; however, it may actually fuel our creativity—crazy as it seems.

Someone said, "The brain is a mass of cranial nerve tissue, most of it in mint condition." That's the bad news. The good news is that, unlike other organs in our body that wear out, the brain gets sharper the more it is used. Moreover, even moderate exercise can increase your mental capacity, as it drives more blood and oxygen to the brain and stimulates the increased production of a chemical that helps repair brain cells.

A Japanese neuroscientist put a group of young people on a jogging program of thirty minutes, two to three times per week. When he tested them at the end of twelve weeks on a series of memory skills, their scores significantly increased, and so did the speed with which they completed the tests. Of equal note, their gains disappeared almost immediately when they stopped jogging.[23]

So, what should we take away from all of this research? In practical terms, it means that a wise pastor will read, study, and plan resolutely —giving the left brain a serious workout; then, intentionally and systematically schedule breaks allowing the Holy Spirit opportunity to guide the creative processes of the right brain. Armed with this vital information, some of you may want to retrofit your office with exercise equipment and a recliner.

"Nothing in this world will ever take the place of preaching except better preaching."[24] I am coming to believe that our good preaching would get much better if we start the left brain preparation early enough to allow the right brain time to add its creativity and "aha" insights. Take me up on this challenge, if you really believe that the *next* sermon you preach could be your best one. Surely, we haven't all been duped into taking those polite front-door compliments about our sermons at face value.

Maximizing pastors recognize that reading is to the mind what exercise is to the body. Read with an open mind—to be stretched, not to be confirmed in your current set of beliefs. With approximately 375,000 new books published annually in the English language[25] (to say nothing of magazines, newspapers, etc.), we could easily drown in a vast sea of information before finding the few volumes that may buoy our ministry. Wide reading may be attractive, but carefully selected reading scratches where we are itching and powers maximum ministry performance. In his devotional book *This Day with the Master*, Dr. Dennis Kinlaw recalls a conversation in which he asked A. W. Tozer about his reading habits and influential books. Tozer offered a surprising answer, delivered with great conviction: "Don't ever read a good book. You don't have time. You will never read all of the best books. For goodness' sake, don't waste your time on a good one!"[26] Solicit reading recommendations from a few trusted friends—academics and practitioners—to find the best books.

FOUR

Moving Beyond Mediocrity

In the musical version of Charles Dickens'
Oliver Twist, there is a pivotal scene in
which the old scoundrel Fagan sings "Can
a Man Change?" It's an important song in
this particular play and one of the most important questions in all of life. Can we
change? Of course we can, if we will. "The
greatest discovery of my generation,"
wrote William James, "is that human

beings *can* alter their lives by altering their attitudes of mind."[1] Henry David Thoreau adds, "I know of no more encouraging fact than the unquestionable ability of man to elevate his life by conscious endeavor."[2] It is one thing for the father of modern psychology and a legendary author to answer our question in the affirmative; it quite another to hear God say, "Yes, you can." I would remind you that the possibility of change, prompted by His grace and facilitated by His Spirit, is what the gospel is all about. Can a person change? God's yes is a recurring theme throughout Scripture. Perhaps that's why Dr. J. G. Morrison (former general superintendent of the Church of the Nazarene) was fond of saying, "What ought to be can be!" He, unlike James and Thoreau, would recognize that life transformation requires the coupling of divine grace and human endeavor. Can a person change? *Yes*—change is both possible and desirable.

Would-be change agents must begin with themselves. But how do we start? Psychologists studying how people change have developed a five-stage model that includes precontemplation, contemplation, preparation, action, and maintenance.[3] I offer a brief summary of each step as a guide to help you determine where you are in regard to my maximizing your ministry challenge.

- Precontemplation: a period of growing unrest in which change is not a conscious concern—if one ignores the nonspecific frustration, this stage can last indefinitely.
- Contemplation: the stage in which one acknowledges a problem and begins to consider its nature, vacillating between wanting to take action and resisting it—recognizable in statements like: "I've got to do something, but I'm not sure that I'm ready" or "Maybe I'll do it someday."
- Preparation: that ramping-up time when you take small, provisional steps and start imagining what your changed life would be like; a person says, "I'm going to do this" and sets dates; the commitment to change may not be evident to others yet.
- Action: the phase when the commitment to change becomes obvious to others via your behavioral differences.

- Maintenance: the stage in which behaviors become habits by repetition and your changed life begins to feel *natural.*

English author Graham Greene wrote, "There is always one moment . . . when the door opens and lets the future in."[4] Maybe, just maybe, that moment has arrived for you. Having pondered the possibilities of your pastoral potential, you may be ready now to let the future in. It's time to escape the maelstrom of mediocrity. Tie yourself to the water cask and jump into the raging waters.

Sir Osbert Sitwell wrote a fanciful novel *The Man Who Lost Himself,* with a memorable scene where the hero was trailing a person in Paris. In an effort to determine whether or not the man he was after was stopping at a certain hotel, he devised a shrewd scheme. The hero would ask the hotel clerk if he himself—giving his own name—was staying there and then sneak a peak at the registry to see if the name of the other man was entered. So he carried out the plan and got the shock of his life. The clerk looked up and said: "Yes, he has been waiting for you in Room 40. I will have you shown right up." At this point, there was nothing to do but go through with it. The man followed the bell boy to Room 40, and it is there that the story goes off the deep end. As he entered the room, the hero found a man remarkably like himself—the person as he would be at the age of 40, just 20 years ahead.[5]

This imaginative novel contains an important kernel of truth: there is a man or woman out there waiting for each of us in the future—the person we will become. Will that person be one who is still spinning around in the maelstrom of mediocrity or will it be one who stands on the shore fondly remembering the ascent? There's a sense in which you can fashion your own future by the choices you are presently making. Do you really want to overcome the factors that contribute to underachievement in your ministry? Are you willing to resign religious work in favor of *Christian* ministry? Can you envision the maximizing pastor you want to be 20 years from now? Are you ready to take the first steps on this long, arduous journey?

SPECIFIC STEPS TOWARD BECOMING A MAXIMIZING PASTOR

1. Prayerfully commit to the process. I suggest you preserve your commitment to change with an Ebenezer stone (any tangible ob-

ject) and place it in a prominent place as a visible reminder of God's presence and help in the process. You will draw inspiration from it down the road.

2. Tell your family and closest friends to expect changes in your life but avoid seeking approval. If you leave them in the dark, they may be puzzled and offended when you no longer meet their familiar expectations. Caution: the deep need for approval may cause you to waver at this point; do not allow this very personal decision to become a referendum.

3. Enlist the support of an accountability partner, preferably someone of the same gender who is on a similar journey. That person's role could be one of a coach, cheerleader, confidant, or whatever fits your purposes. I recommend someone who can be both tough and tender. Grant him or her the freedom to get in your face when you plateau or get distracted from the maximizing mind-set. You'll also need lots of encouragement to keep you from throwing in the towel. To avoid being trapped in an uncomfortable or unproductive arrangement, you should begin on a trial basis. Clearly communicate mutual expectations and meet weekly or at least monthly for progress reports.

4. Create a pleasant and functional workspace. Considering the nature and amount of work done in the pastor's study, it should be among the most attractive rooms in the church building, with adequate lighting, comfortable furnishings, and ready access to the tools of your trade (books, computer, etc.). In short, the space should be designed to beckon you there and to support your efforts.

5. Continually seek God's vision for your ministry. There are many things in life that will catch your eye, but only a few will catch your heart. When God gives you a passion for something, pursue it with fervency.

6. Organize your life around priorities. One way to measure the effectiveness of a leader is to take note of those things he or she leaves undone. Establish behavioral routines that are congruent with your purpose, priorities, and goals, but be flexible enough to embrace ministry opportunities within God's timing. On a broader

scale, some have made good use of timelines whereby a person charts the course of his or her desired future, noting major steps and dates along the way.

7. Avoid "idle curiosities" (Emerson's term) and "soft addictions" (Judith Wright's term). They rob us of time, drain our energy, numb our feelings, and keep us from optimal living. Warning: because these addictions are socially acceptable, even within church circles, they are often the most difficult to release.

8. Conduct an honest self-appraisal, noting your strengths and weaknesses. Self-awareness is fundamental to self-improvement. Take inventory of your current relationship with God, people connections, physical condition, work habits, spiritual gifts, passions, education, skills set, goals, character flaws, self-defeating habits, rationalizations, and so on.

9. Address the deficiencies (relationship issues, character issues, lack of required skills for effective pastoral work, etc.). Remember that Rome wasn't built in a day . . . these adjustments will take lots of time, energy, and patience. Some may require formal education and counseling.

10. Acknowledge your progress, especially in the earliest stages of change. Where we are in relation to our potential is not nearly as important as the direction in which we are headed. The longest, most challenging journey begins with a single step. Rejoice in what God has enabled you to do early on and refrain from focusing on how far you need to go.

11. Watch your language. Research confirms that our spoken and written words can either reinforce our self-limiting behaviors or aid in our liberation from them. Engage in positive self-talk and language that embraces personal responsibility.

12. Participate in best-practices peer learning opportunities. Woe unto us, if we ever reach the place where we feel as though we cannot learn from our colleagues—even those who are less experienced or less educated. Iron sharpens iron. Whenever we cooperate, we usually draw out the best in one another; whenever we compete, we usually draw out the worst in one another.

13. Humbly give God the glory whenever you begin to stand out among your peers. "It is while we are being good that we have the chance of being really bad," says Eugene Peterson. "It is in the course of being a good pastor that we have the most chance of developing pastoral *hubris*—pride, arrogance, and insensitivity."[6] Do not be ruined by the praise of people nor devastated by their criticism.

14. Become a mentor for someone else who refuses to settle for mediocrity. Optimal ministry is contagious. As other like-minded pastors approach you, pour yourself into them. At the end of the day, there really is no success without successors.

Change is not easy, because it feels so unnatural. Not long ago, I accidentally stripped the skin off my left wrist while pressure cleaning our house—a bonehead act that led to the temporary transfer of my watch to the right arm. This minor adjustment caused me major frustration. I kept instinctively looking at my left wrist for the time of day—a habit developed over decades. Much to my surprise, however, the position of my watch started to feel natural after two weeks or so.

It's your life. It's your only one, unless you decide to create a second life in the cyberworld of the Internet. You can continue in the same self-limiting patterns because they feel natural, or you can embrace changes that lead to a more fulfilling and fruitful ministry in the real world. If you decide to make the leap, it may feel as if you are living someone else's life for a while. Stay the course. Resist the temptation to return to the old rut. Before long, maximizing ministry feels normal.

FIVE

Father's Approval

Paul Harvey said, "You can tell you're on the road to success; it's uphill all the way!"[1] Each step in the maximizing ministry journey requires discipline and hard work, making it the "road less traveled." Those who dare to walk in this direction need something to keep them motivated when the going gets tough and they are tempted to turn back. That inspirational "something" just may be our knowledge of the benefits—both temporal and eternal—that are inextricably linked to optimal ministry. Remember: if you don't scale the mountain, you won't see the view. The rewards far outweigh the risks. These include but certainly are not limited to the following:

A BROADER AND DEEPER INFLUENCE UPON OTHERS

We are in the most rewarding business of all. Just think about it, God has chosen us to partner with Him in life transformations—"extreme makeovers" from the inside out. We should be both humbled and motivated by the idea that the quality of our work has some bearing on how many find their way into the kingdom of God and the degree to which they are aligned with its values. For us, the bottom line is more and better disciples of Jesus Christ. That is our Master's clear message, and we shouldn't allow anyone else to define success for us.

Beware annual reports, the primary instrument for measuring ministry effectiveness in most churches. I have found these forms to be woefully inadequate, not because they ask the *wrong* questions but because they seldom ask enough of the *right* questions. In addition to the queries about how many people came to church and how much money they contributed, annual reports would become better diagnostic tools if they revealed the spiritual disciplines of church members, the number who are actively engaged in an ongoing ministry, their efforts to befriend the unchurched, and their interest in passing the faith along to the next generation. Please understand that I have no problem with counting nickels and noses. Statistics are important gauges, but they certainly do not tell the whole story. In fact, they may even distort reality and lull us into a false sense of accomplishment—thus keeping us from realizing our full potential. A good pastor may enable the church to reach its ecclesiastical goals; the maximizing pastor keeps them in proper perspective and understands that these are but wood, hay, and stubble compared to the redemptive influence he or she has upon others. It is all about adding value to their lives.

Most of us want God to expand our influence. It is remarkable how, in some circles, the prayer of Jabez has virtually replaced the prayer of

Jesus as the pattern. I have an uncomfortable feeling that far too many pastors have been reciting it in hopes that God would "enlarge their territory" by moving them to a bigger and better church. Have you considered the possibility that He could enlarge your territory without a transfer? The good news is that our sphere of influence expands as we boldly face the factors that contribute to underachievement and set out to maximize our potential. In a sense, then, we can hasten the answer to our petition for expanded influence. Growing pastors tend to lead growing churches.

I want to be crystal clear at this point: maximizing our ministry must not be mistaken for growing a larger congregation, although it may very well result in numerical increases because one who demonstrates faithfulness over a few things can be trusted with many things (see Matt. 25:14-30; Luke 19:11-27). However, growth is both quantitative and qualitative. Our mission is to make disciples—authentic followers of Jesus Christ who are deeply rooted in scriptural soil.

Pastors often bemoan the spiritual immaturity of those milk-drinking, spiritual infants who have been on the way (or in the way) for decades. We offer them the meat of the Word through various delivery systems (Sunday School, discipleship classes, small-group meetings, etc.), but in many cases, nothing seems to work. Our futile, force-feeding efforts have been aimed at *them*. At the risk of sounding naive, I want to offer a novel approach that shifts the focus from them to you. Concentrate on getting spiritually aligned, relationally connected, physically energized, and mentally focused for the next six months. God will use the new you to improve the ethos of the congregation. Try it and see what happens. I predict that you will make the delightful discovery that when you really get your own house in order, others will follow your lead into balanced wholeness under the Lordship of Christ. Growing pastors tend to lead growing disciples.

Why? The answer is tucked away in the following vignette from the life of Donald Miller:

> I never liked jazz music because jazz music doesn't resolve. But I was outside the Bagdad Theater in Portland one night when I saw a man playing the saxophone. I stood there for fifteen minutes, and

he never opened his eyes. After that I liked jazz music. Sometimes you have to watch somebody love something before you can love it yourself. It is as if they are showing you the way.[2]

Maximizing pastors make a priceless contribution to everyone around them by simply being the living incarnation of what we preach and teach. As congregants watch us loving something or someone, their desire to do the same grows exponentially.

THE PERSONAL SENSE OF SATISFACTION

Most of us are familiar with Abraham Maslow's hierarchy of needs proposed in his 1943 paper titled *A Theory of Human Motivation* and often depicted as a pyramid consisting of five levels. The four lower levels (physiological, safety, love/belonging, and esteem) are grouped together as *deficiency needs*; the top level consists of self-actualization and self-transcendence, commonly called the *being needs*. Maslow's theory asserts that as humans meet their basic needs, they seek to satisfy successively higher needs that occupy a set hierarchy.

Being needs drive behavior. *Self-actualization* is that instinctual need to make the most of our unique abilities. According to Maslow, "A musician must make music, the artist must paint, a poet must write, if he is to be ultimately at peace with himself. What a man can be, he must be."[3] *Self-transcendence,* the term Maslow tentatively placed at the pinnacle of his hierarchy, involves connecting to something beyond the ego or to helping others find self-fulfillment and realize their potential. I am not quite sure where these terms fit into our theological constructs, but it seems that the Creator has hardwired us for both self-actualization and self-transcendence. Joy is God's precious gift to those who are committed to maximizing their potential and helping others to do the same. That explains why the writing of this book has been such a delight, not a duty.

Fruitfulness is fun. A psychologist at Stanford University demonstrated how we are driven by productivity. The researcher hired a logger and said, "I'll pay you double what you get paid at the logging camp, if you'll take the blunt end of this axe and just pound this log all day. You never have to cut one piece of wood . . . simply hit the log as hard as you can just as you would do if you were logging." The man worked half a day and quit. The psychologist asked why. The logger replied, "Because every time I swing an axe, I have to see the chips fly. If I don't see the chips fly, it's no fun."[4]

Maximizing pastors who are seeing the chips fly could never be lured away from their calling by more money. Why? Because joy, the emotional by-product of fruitful ministry, is priceless.

FEWER REGRETS AT THE END OF THE JOURNEY

In his book titled *Why Not the Best?* President Jimmy Carter recalls the day when he had applied for the nuclear submarine program and the legendary Admiral Hyman Rickover was interviewing him for the job.

> He let me choose any subjects I wished to discuss. Very carefully, I chose those about which I knew most at the time . . . and he began to ask me a series of questions of increasing difficulty. Finally, he asked me . . . "How did you stand in your class at the Naval Academy?" I answered, "Sir, I stood fifty-ninth in a class of 820." I sat back to wait for the congratulations which never came. Instead, the question, "Did you do your best?" I started to say, "Yes, sir," but I remembered who this was, and recalled several of the many times at the Academy when I could have learned more about our allies, our enemies, weapons, strategy, and so forth . . . I finally said, "no, sir, I didn't always do my best." He looked at me for a long time, and then asked one final question which I have never been able to forget—or to answer. He said, "Why not?"[5]

No one knows what questions we will face when life's hourglass is empty and we stand before the Lord, but it wouldn't surprise me to hear Him ask, "Did you do your best?" and "Why not?" If that happens, each of us will be hard-pressed to justify our shouldas, couldas, wouldas.

Now let's face it. We are human; regrets are inevitable. But it makes no sense to dwell on the if onlys, because there's very little we can do to correct the blunders of our past. Let them go.

Nonetheless, we can and should strive to minimize our regrets from this point onward. That's more likely to happen when we keep our mortality in mind. That's not as easy as it sounds, since we reside in a death-denying culture. Have you noticed the way we fight the aging process, sanitize death with our euphemisms, and send people away to die? It seems as if most people are living for today with little or no thought about tomorrow. All of us could learn something from King Philip II of Macedonia, father of Alexander the Great, who ordered one of his servants to come to him every morning and declare loudly, "Remember, Philip, that you must die." The simplest way to avoid regrets is to live as if you were dying. Let's face it—the prospect of death has a way of bringing our priorities into their proper order.

There's a distinct difference between existing and living. I want to *live* until I die. Wouldn't you agree? If we do, there will be fewer regrets at the end of the road.

Arthur Berry committed as many as 150 burglaries and stole jewels valued at between five and ten million dollars. He became known as the "gentleman thief" because he seldom robbed from anyone who was not listed in the social register and often committed his crimes wearing a tuxedo. On an occasion or two, when caught in the act by a victim, he even charmed his way out of being reported or turned over to the police. He was eventually caught, convicted, and sent to prison for 25 years. After Berry was released, a newspaper reporter interviewed him. He recounted the thrilling episodes of his life in crime, and ended the interview with this sobering statement: "I am not good at morals. But, early in my life I was intelligent and clever, and got along well with people. I think I could have made something of life. But, I didn't. So, when you write the story of my life, when you tell people about all the burglaries, don't leave the big one out. Don't just tell them I robbed Jesse Livermore, the Wall Street baron, or the cousin of the king of England. You tell them Arthur Berry robbed Arthur Berry! I stole the most from myself."[6]

Whenever we sleepwalk through life and just meet our basic obligations, we rob others who would benefit from our ministry; however, we may steal the most from ourselves. John Greenleaf Whittier's couplet comes to mind:

> *For of all sad words of tongue or pen;*
> *The saddest are these: "It might have been!"*[7]

The rewards of optimal ministry include the broader and deeper influence upon others, a personal sense of satisfaction, and fewer regrets at the end of our journey; however, these pale in comparison to . . .

HEARING THE MASTER SAY,
"WELL DONE, GOOD AND FAITHFUL SERVANT"

Like so many men of his generation, my father struggled to verbally express affection and affirmation. I am sure he loved me and took pride in me; he just wouldn't say so. My workaholic and perfectionist tendencies could probably be traced to a deep, subconscious desire for his approval. Dad's gone now, but I still seek his blessing.

The void in my heart was partially filled by Dad's handwritten note drafted near the end of his life. It is a priceless possession—short and sweet. He wrote, "While I'm in good mind I want to say how much I'm proud of you and your family . . . your Mom and I have raised a fine set of kids . . . we did our best in giving you a heritage to be proud of . . . continue to be Dad's fine preacher boy and give Satan the knockout punch." You can imagine the flood of emotion that engulfed me as I read these words for the first time just days after his passing. I reread them often.

Months later, God granted a dream in which Dad gave me three precious gifts—a warm embrace, a kiss on the cheek, and the assurance of his love. It was so real. To this day, I cannot speak of it with dry eyes.

A note and a dream—what else could I want? Friends, I anticipate that great reunion day when my dream becomes reality and both of my fathers welcome me home saying, "Well done, good and faithful servant."

Poe's story *A Descent into the Maelstrom* contains anecdotal references that underscore the sweeping strength of the current. The narrator mentions whales that were overpowered and a bear "borne down" while attempting to swim from Lofoden to Moskoe. He roared so loudly that he was heard on shore! These robust creatures underestimated the power of those rushing waters.

Could it be that we have underestimated the maelstrom of mediocrity? Freed from "sin's dread sway," are we now held captive by the spirit of this age? If so, let's tie ourselves to the water cask and rise to fulfill God's destiny for our lives. Warning: the upward journey may terrify us at times, to the point where our hair turns white or turns loose! In the end, however, we can stand on the mountain and tell others about God's enablement in our ascent from the maelstrom. They will be left to draw their own conclusions about the credibility of our story.

Appendix 1

I. To Be a Better Person

    A. Spiritually. In an effort to maintain an intimate relationship with God, I will . . .

        1. Spend the first 30 minutes of each day in Bible reading, prayer, and journaling.

        2. Use Kinlaw's *This Day with the Master* (Grand Rapids: Zondervan, 2002) for daily meditations.

        3. Adopt a plan to read the entire Bible devotionally.

        4. Fast one meal per week.

        5. Meet one hour per week with my accountability/prayer partner.

        6. Listen to praise and worship music while driving alone.

    B. Physically. In an effort to care for my body (the temple of the Holy Spirit), I will . . .

        1. Walk on the treadmill 45 minutes, at least five days per week.

        2. Keep my cholesterol count below 200 . . . take Lipitor daily, avoid red meat, and so forth.

        3. Get at least seven hours of sleep daily.

        4. Slow my pace, taking time to smell the roses.

        5. Take off one day per week for golfing, fishing, and so forth.

        6. Lose 15 pounds and keep my weight below 180 pounds.

    C. Emotionally. In an effort to develop a winsome personality, I will . . .

        1. Cultivate an attitude of gratitude, intentionally thanking God and others for their gracious acts.

        2. Be authentic and transparent.

        3. Recapture some of the playfulness of my youth.

        4. Immediately forgive those who injure my spirit.

---

*This personal goals form is offered as an example and not intended to reflect an exhaustive listing of a pastor's ministry responsibilities. They vary, of course, in each setting. Once listed in this fashion, the goals should be integrated into one's weekly schedule (Appendix 2). Both Appendixes 1 and 2 are used by permission of Dr. Bill Burch.

D. Mentally. In an effort to grow mentally as a lifelong learner, I will . . .

    1. Develop a diverse reading program based upon book recommendations from trusted friends. Digest at least two books per week.

    2. Improve my Spanish by listening to the audio CDs.

    3. Take regular breaks during intense projects.

    4. Watch television news at least once daily, noting national and international events.

    5. Attend a writer's seminar.

E. Financially. In an effort to practice whole-life stewardship, I will . . .

    1. Invest $____ weekly in Kingdom work through storehouse tithing and offerings.

    2. Contribute $____ per month toward our TSA (tax-sheltered annuity).

    3. Pay off the car loan by the end of the year.

II. To Be a Better Partner

In an effort to enhance my loving relationship with Debbie, I will . . .

    1. Express my love and appreciation for her daily in various ways.

    2. Encourage her in the development and expression of her spiritual gifts.

    3. Be in the moment when we engage in conversations.

    4. Rediscover the joy of table games.

    5. Schedule a special evening out at least once a week.

    6. Take Debbie to Whitestone Bed-n-Breakfast.

III. To Be a Better Parent

In an effort to enhance my loving relationship with Drew, I will . . .

    1. Verbally express my love for him on a regular basis . . . on the phone and face-to-face.

    2. Inquire about his relationship with the Lord on a regular basis.

    3. Pray daily for him.

    4. Provide counsel, whenever it's requested.

    5. Schedule an annual father-son outing.

    6. Give him Dave Ramsey's books on money management.

IV. To Be a Better Professional

In an effort to shepherd the flock, I will . . .

A. As Pastor

1. Call every church member on his or her birthday to express love and appreciation.
2. Intentionally engage in redemptive conversations on social occasions.
3. Visit in the homes of first-time attenders within a week.
4. Connect with at least 20 families/individuals per week (visits, meals, outings, e-mails, etc.).
5. Visit the hospitalized once per week, in cooperation with other staff and laity.
6. Provide counseling on a limited basis (spiritual, marriage, pre-marriage, etc.).
7. Pray daily for members of the church.
8. Teach a lay shepherds class.
9. Administer the sacrament of the Lord's Supper monthly.

B. As Administrator

In an effort to guide the church in the fulfillment of its mission, I will . . .

1. Lead weekly pastoral staff meetings.
2. Oversee the work on the Policies and Procedures Manual.
3. Conduct staff consultations monthly and formal evaluations annually.
4. Report to the church board monthly.
5. Work closely with the finance committee in the development of an annual budget.
6. Plan a church board retreat to focus on vision, team building, and so forth.
7. Lead the nominating committee prior to annual meeting.
8. Provide input for the weekly bulletin, monthly e-newsletter, and Web site.

C. As Preacher

In an effort to faithfully proclaim God's Word, I will . . .

1. Prepare at least one new sermon each week.
2. Listen to or read three sermons from excellent communicators.
3. Enhance my messages with PowerPoint and other visual aids.

4. Attempt to preach without dependency on notes.
5. Solicit feedback on my messages from my prayer/accountability partner.
6. Purge my sermons of coded and stained-glass language.

Appendix 2

WEEKLY CALENDAR*

	Sunday	Monday	Tuesday	Wednesday	Thursday	Friday	Saturday
Morning	"Me time"	"Me time"	"Me time"	"Me time"	"Me time"	"Me time"	"Me time"
	A.M. Worship	Treadmill (45 min.) Golf	Treadmill (45 min.) Pastoral staff meeting	Treadmill (45 min.) Mentoring pastoral interns Hospital visits	Treadmill (45 min.) Sermon preparation	Treadmill (45 min.) Administrative work Sermon preparation	Treadmill (45 min.) Phone calls Reading
	Lunch	Lunch	Lunch	Lunch	Lunch	Lunch	Lunch
Afternoon	Rest/relaxation	Relaxation/Shopping with Debbie	Begin sermon preparation Correspondence Prepare board report	Meet with Larry, my accountability prayer partner Administrative work Long-range planning	Zone Pastors' meeting Administrative work Staff consultation Premarriage counseling	Meeting with TNU personnel Counseling session PowerPoint presentation	Visit newcomers, members Yard work
	Dinner	Dinner	Dinner	Dinner	Dinner	Dinner	Dinner
Evening	P.M. Service	Reading	Board meeting	Pastoral visits Reading	Dinner with a church family TNU basketball game	Family night	Relax at home/Review sermon

*Used by permission of Dr. Bill Burch.

Chapter "Takeaways"

(Note: The following "takeaways" are offered in hopes that they will assist the reader in making personal applications from the text. They also could serve as a discussion guide for a group of pastors committed to making the leap together.)

Chapter 1: "The Maelstrom of Mediocrity"

1. On a scale of 1 to 10, identify where you are in regard to the fulfillment of your ministry potential.

2. Review the following list of tendencies and put a check mark to the left of each one that you see in yourself. Ask your spouse to identify the tendencies seen in you and record that evaluation in the right column.

____ inconsistent or insufficient effort   ____
____ a lack of real engagement   ____
____ ambivalence in decision-making   ____
____ lack of follow-through   ____
____ disorganization   ____
____ inability to reach goals   ____
____ quitting just before achieving success   ____
____ procrastination   ____
____ involvement in work that doesn't stretch you   ____
____ a fear of failure   ____

3. Which of Kenneth Christian's self-limiting styles best describes you?

Chapter 2: "Good Is Not Good Enough"

1. Define your calling in 25 words or less.

2. Prayerfully identify those who have injured your spirit and seek God's guidance in the restoration of those relationships.

3. Place the written understandings between you and the church board on the agenda for your next meeting.

4. Identify the soft addictions in your life and develop a goals-oriented weekly schedule. (Appendixes 1 and 2 may be helpful at this point.)

5. Create a space where you can enjoy uninterrupted devotional moments on a daily basis and identify two or three firelighters who stoke your spiritual passion.

6. Make an extensive list of your positive attributes.

7. Paint a word picture of the ministry setting in which you would like to be 10 years from now and ponder the question: Does this represent selfish or sanctified ambition?

8. Contact your regional college/university about learning opportunities.

9. Introduce one out of the boat initiative to your lay leaders within the next three months and kill at least one passé church program.

10. Refine your out-of-the-boat idea with a discussion group of six trusted laypersons, listening carefully for the messages behind their words.

11. If nepotism has fostered jealousy and cynicism in your heart, confess it now and seek God's forgiveness. If you are related or otherwise connected to someone who has had a positive influence upon your ministry, express sincere appreciation to that person.

12. Get a thorough physical examination and ask your doctor for specific suggestions related to coping with vocational stress.

13. Review your ministerial track record, noting your tenure in each assignment and the reason for your departure.

14. Compare your salary to the average figures revealed in the text and talk with your district or regional leader if you need assistance in raising awareness among lay leaders.

15. Dialogue with your spouse about her or his feelings related to life in the ministry.

Chapter 3: "A 1st-Century Model for 21st-Century Ministry"

1. List the three individuals who have done more than anyone else to shape your ministry and briefly describe their particular contribution.

2. The author lists six characteristics of *Christian* ministry. What others would you add to his list?

3. Perform a behind-the-scenes act of service for someone outside the church, noting his or her response and your feelings during the process.

4. Prepare an obedience sermon or Bible study from the Gospel of John, noting how Jesus enlists the cooperation of others in the performance of miracles.

5. Read or reread *Christian Excellence* by Jon Johnston (Kansas City: Nazarene Publishing House, 1985).

6. Plan an overnight spiritual retreat within the next six months.

7. Think creatively about how, where, and when you can connect with unchurched people.

8. Prayerfully choose an accountability/prayer partner and begin meeting weekly.

Chapter 4: "Moving Beyond Mediocrity"

1. Where are you in regard to the maximizing ministry challenge?

Precontemplation	Contemplation	Preparation	Action	Maintenance

2. Describe the person you would like to be 20 years from now.

3. What's keeping you from fully embracing optimal ministry today?

Chapter 5: "Father's Approval"

1. The author's list of rewards for maximizing ministry includes: the difference we make in others' lives, the personal sense of satisfaction, fewer regrets at the end of the journey, and hearing our Father's approval. Are there others?

2. Display an Ebenezer stone in your office as a visible reminder of God's enablement in the process of becoming all you can be.

Notes

Introduction

1. Scott Wright, "NFL Draft Countdown," www.nfldraftcountdown.com (April 2005).

2. Anna Quindlen, "Mom, Dad and Abortion," Public and Private, *New York Times*, sec. 4, July 1, 1990.

3. William Willimon, *Pastor: The Theology and Practice of Ordained Ministry* (Nashville: Abingdon Press, 2002), 326.

4. *ThinkExist.com Quotations Online*, s.v. "Harry Emerson Fosdick Quotes," http://thinkexist.com/quotes/harry_emerson_fosdick (accessed January 4, 2007).

Chapter 1

1. Edgar Allan Poe, "In a Maelstrom," in *Carpenter's Penny Book* (London, 1841).

2. *Time* (June 20, 1983), quoted in Florence Littauer (Eugene, Oreg.: Harvest House Publishers, 1983).

3. Jim Loehr and Tony Schwartz, *The Power of Full Engagement: Managing Energy, Not Time, Is the Key to High Performance and Personal Renewal* (New York: Free Press, 2005), 5-6.

4. See Richard C. Schiming, "Grade Inflation Article," Minnesota State University, http://www.mnsu.edu/cetl/teachingresources/articles/gradeinflation.html (accessed January 4, 2007).

5. Kenneth W. Christian, *Your Own Worst Enemy: Breaking the Habit of Adult Underachievement* (New York: HarperCollins, 2002), 21-30. Used by permission.

Chapter 2

1. Jim Collins, *Good to Great* (New York: HarperCollins, 2001), 1, 13.

2. Warren Bennis and Robert Townsend, *Reinventing Leadership: Strategies to Empower the Organization* (New York: William Morrow and Co., 1995), 161.

3. "Misdirected Calls," Net Results <www.netresults.org>.

4. Os Guinness, *The Call: Finding and Fulfilling the Central Purpose of Your Life* (Nashville: Thomas Nelson, 1998), 44.

5. John A. Stroman, *Thunder from the Mountain* (Nashville: Upper Room, 1990), 28-29.

6. Attributed to Louise Bush-Brown, Bartleby.com, http://www.bartleby.com/73/458.html (paraphrased by author; accessed January 4, 2007).

7. Thomas à Kempis, *The Imitation of Christ* (Milwaukee: Bruce Publishing Co., 1940), 16.

8. C. S. Lewis, *The Four Loves* (New York: Harcourt, Brace and World, Inc., 1960), 169.

9. William McCumber, *Herald of Holiness* (October 15, 1987).

10. Marshall Shelley, *Well-Intentioned Dragons: Ministering to Problem People in the Church* (Waco: Word Books, 1985), 42.

11. Eugene H. Peterson, *Under the Unpredictable Plant: An Exploration in Vocational Holiness* (Grand Rapids: William B. Eerdmans, 1992), 157.

12. Henri Nouwen, *The Wounded Healer* (New York: Doubleday, 1979).

13. Alan Alda, *Never Have Your Dog Stuffed* (New York: Random House, 2005).

14. Jack Hayford, *Taking Hold of Tomorrow* (Ventura: Regal Books, 1989), 36.

15. William Willimon, *Worship as Pastoral Care* (Nashville: Abingdon Press, 1979), chap. 9.

16. Willimon, *Pastor*, 63.

17. *The Barna Update* (September 25, 2001).

18. Harriet Braiker, *The Disease to Please* (New York: McGraw-Hill, 2001).

19. Willimon, *Pastor,* 60.

20. Henri Nouwen, *Making All Things New* (San Francisco: HarperSan Francisco, 1981), 24.

21. Jill Andresky Fraser, *White Collar Sweatshop: The Deterioration of Work and Its Reward in Corporate America* (New York: W. W. Norton and Co., 2001), 20.

22. Paul McFedries, *Word Spy: The Word Lover's Guide to Modern Culture* (New York: Broadway Books, 2004), 36.

23. Judith Wright, *There Must Be More than This: Finding More Life, Love, and Meaning by Overcoming Your Soft Addictions* (New York: Broadway Books, 2003).

24. A. A. Milne, *The Complete Tales of Winnie-the-Pooh* (New York: Dutton Children's Books, 1994), 157-58.

25. Bob Moorehead, *Words Aptly Spoken* (Kirkland, Wash.: Overlake Christian Press, 1995), 99. Used by permission.

26. "The Quotable Wesley," The United Church of Canada, http://www.united-church .ca/wesley/quotes.shtm.

27. Attributed to C. H. Mackintosh in H. A. Ironside, *Sailing with Paul* (1913; reprint, Bedford, Pa.: Moments With the Book, 1990), 53.

28. John Maxwell, *Your Road Map for Success: You Can Get There from Here* (Nashville: Thomas Nelson, 2002), 37.

29. Arthur Gordon, *Touch of Wonder* (Old Tappan: Fleming H. Revell, 1978), 45-46.

30. Florence Littauer, *It Takes So Little to Be Above Average* (Eugene: Harvest House Publishers, 1983), 10.

31. Larry McKain, "Maintaining Holy Ambition" in *NCS Weekly Insights,* an e-mail devotional sent to New Church Specialities partners on January 14, 2005.

32. Gary McCord, *Just a Range Ball in a Box of Titleists* (New York: The Berkley Publishing Group, 1998).

33. Ken Cohen, "The Real McCord," http://www.protourgolfers.com/ (Sept. 12, 2005).

34. The Wesleyan Church, *Manual of Ministry Preparation* (Indianapolis: The General Department of Education and the Ministry, 2004) par. 621.

35. *The United Methodist Book of Discipline* (Nashville: Abingdon Press, 2005) par. 351.2.

36. Bruce Larson, *There's a Lot More to Health than Not Being Sick* (Waco, Tex: Word Books, 1981), 31.

37. John Ortberg, *If You Want to Walk on Water, You've Got to Get Out of the Boat* (Grand Rapids: Zondervan, 2001), 9-10.

38. Rosalene Glickman, *Optimal Thinking* (New York: John Wiley and Sons, 2002), 66.

39. James Joyce, The Quotation Page, http://www.quotationspage.com/quote/3103.html (accessed January 5, 2007).

40. Perry Buffington, *Forgive and Forget* (Universal Press Syndicate, 8-29-99). The Zeigarnik effect is named for Russian psychologist Bluma Zeigarnik who described the phenomenon in 1927.

41. Paul Borden, *Hit the Bullseye: How Denominations Can Aim the Congregation at the Mission Field* (Nashville: Abingdon Press, 2003).

42. Robert Townsend, *Up the Organization* (New York: Alfred Knopf, 1970), 93.

43. *The Gleaner* (Kingston, Jamaica, February 16, 2003).

44. Robert N. Bellah, et al., *Habits of the Heart: Individualism and Commitment in American Life* (Berkley and Los Angeles: University of California Press, 1985).

45. Collins, *Good to Great*, 77.

46. Dietrich Bonhoeffer, *Dietrich Bonhoeffer Works Vol. 5, Life Together and Prayerbook of the Bible*, ed. Geffrey B. Kelly, trans. Daniel W. Bloesch and James H. Burtness (Minneapolis: Fortress Press, 1996), 36.

47. Collins, *Good to Great*, 74-77.

48. John Maxwell, "The Value of Shared Thinking," *Leadership Wired*, Vol. 5, Issue 20 (Nov. 15, 2002).

49. Adam Bellow, *In Praise of Nepotism: A Natural History* (New York: Doubleday, 2003).

50. McFedries, *Word Spy*, 29.

51. Rick Riding's Ph.D. dissertation presented to Vanderbilt University is referenced in Mark Graham's *Herald of Holiness* article "Chestnut Ridge—A Ministry for Ministers," (p. 11) dated June 1995. It's also referenced in Dan Spait's *The Time Bomb in the Church: Defusing Pastoral Burnout* (Beacon Hill Press of Kansas City, 1999), 71.

52. James Gleick, *Faster: The Acceleration of Just About Everything* (New York: Pantheon Books, 1999), 27.

53. "The Couch Potato Workout" is outlined in an article dated January 15, 2004, on www.apta.org, The American Physical therapy Association's official web site. No author cited.

54. Carol Hazard, "Snooze You Lose: Top Executives Defy the Rules on Sleep Deprivation," *Richmond-Times Dispatch* (July 23, 2001).

55. Peter Wagner, "Breaking the 100-200 Barrier Seminar" sponsored by the Fuller Institute, March 10, 1994, Indianapolis.

56. Jason Schachter, "What Moves Americans to Move?" Census Bureau, www.usgov info.about.com.

57. ChristianityToday.com/Your Church, "Profile of Today's Pastor: Transitions," John C. LaRue Jr. (June 1995).

58. *The Barna Update* (September 25, 2001).

59. Peterson, *Under the Unpredictable Plant*, 22.

60. Frederick Buechner, *Wishful Thinking* (San Francisco: HarperSanFrancisco, 1993), 119.

61. ChristianityToday.com/Your Church, "Profile of Today's Pastor: Transitions," John C. LaRue Jr. (June 1995).

62. *The Barna Update* (May 28, 2002).

63. Pensions and Benefits, Church of the Nazarene.

64. Christianity Today.com/Your Church, "Pastors and Salary Satisfaction," John C. LaRue Jr. (June 1998).

65. H. B. London, Foreword to *She Can't Even Play the Piano!* Comp. Joyce Williams (Kansas City: Beacon Hill Press of Kansas City, 2005), 11.

66. Ibid., Introduction, 13.

Chapter 3

1. Hannah Whithall Smith, *The Christian's Secret of a Happy Life* (Grand Rapids: Fleming H. Revell, 1952), 215.

2. Don Wellman, *Dynamics of Discipling* (Kansas City: Beacon Hill Press of Kansas City, 1984), 259.

3. Thomas J. Peters and Robert H. Waterman Jr., *In Search of Excellence: Lessons from America's Best-Run Companies* (New York: Harper and Row, 1982).

4. Jon Johnston, *Christian Excellence: Alternative to Success* (Kansas City: Nazarene Publishing House, 1985), 33.

5. R. W. Livingstone, *Greek Ideals and Modern Life* (London: Oxford University Press, n.d.), 69-72.

6. Johnston, *Christian Excellence*, 39.

7. This Associated Press story dated July 8, 2005, was posted on AOL News.

8. William Barclay, *The Gospel of Luke* (Philadelphia: Westminster Press, 1956), 206.

9. Ibid., 207.

10. John Nolland, *Word Biblical Commentary*, Vol. 35B (Nashville: Nelson, 1995), 701.

11. *ThinkExist.com Quotations Online*, s.v. "P. T. Forsyth quotes," http://en.thinkexist.com/quotes/p.t._forsyth/ (accessed January 5, 2007).

12. Mark Middleton, "Obsessed with Doing" in *Lead On, Arrow Leadership News* (November 2000).

13. William Osler in David Michael Martin Rader, "Biography of Sir William Osler," John P. McGovern Academy of Oslerian Medicine, http://www.utmb.edu/osler/about-osler/osler-biography.shtm (accessed January 5, 2007).

14. Ronald Dunn, *Any Christian Can!* (Kalamazoo, Mich.: Master's Press, 1976), 77.

15. *Men of Integrity*, Vol. 1, No. 1.

16. Stephen Covey, *The Seven Habits of Highly Effective People* (New York: Simon and Schuster), 188-99.

17. Ordination ritual, Church of the Nazarene.

18. *ThinkExist.com Quotations Online*, s.v. "Dag Hammarskjöld quotes," http://en.thinkexist.com/quotes/dag_hammarskjold/3.html (accessed January 5, 2007).

19. Loehr and Schwartz, *Power of Full Engagement*, 50-51.

20. Ibid., 56.

21. Ibid., 61.

22. Michael Gelb, *How to Think Like Leonardo da Vinci* (New York: Dell, 1998), 160.

23. Loehr and Schwartz, *Power of Engagement*, 101.

24. Paul Shearer, "We Have This Treasure," lectures at Yale on preaching.

25. "English-Speaking Countries Published 375,000 New books Worldwide in 2004," Bowker.com, http://www.bowker.com/press/bowker/2005_1012_bowker.htm (accessed January 5, 2007).

26. Dennis Kinlaw, *This Day with the Master* (Grand Rapids: Zondervan, 2002), June 10.

Chapter 4

1. See About Quotations, http://quotations.about.com/od/stillmorefamouspeople/a/WilliamJames2.htm.

2. See World of Quotes.com, http://www.worldofquotes.com/author/Henry-David-Thoreau/1/index.html.

3. J. O. Prochaska, C. C. DiClemente, and J. C. Norcross, "In Search of How People Change," in *American Psychologist* 47, 1102-14.

4. See BrainyQuote.com, http://www.brainyquote.com/quotes/authors/g/graham_green.html (accessed January 5, 2007).

5. Halford E. Luccock, *Unfinished Business* (New York: Harper and Brothers, 1956).

6. Peterson, *Under the Unpredictable Plant*, 31.

Chapter 5

1. Quoted by John Maxwell in "Personal Growth," Leadership Wired, http://www.injoy.com/newsletters/leadership/content/issues/9_3/default.htm (accessed January 5, 2007).

2. Donald Miller, *Blue Like Jazz: Nonreligious Thoughts on Christian Spirituality* (Nashville: Nelson, 2003), ix.

3. Abraham Maslow, *Motivation and Personality* (New York: Harper and Brothers, 1954), 91.

4. John Maxwell, *Be All You Can Be: A Challenge to Stretch to Your God-Given Potential* (Wheaton, Ill.: Victor Books, 1987), 21.

5. Jimmy Carter, *Why Not the Best?* (New York: Broadman Press, 1975), 59.

6. Paul W. Powell, *Taking the Stew Out of Stewardship* (Annuity Board of the Southern Baptist Convention, n.d.), 134-35.

7. John Greenleaf Whittier, "Maud Muller," *One Hundred Choice Selections,* ed. Phineas Garrett (Philadelphia: Penn Publishing Co., 1897).

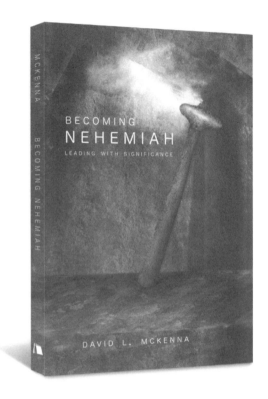

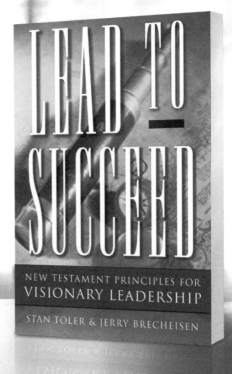

Think on These Things contains meditations that will challenge you to reach your full potential as a leader and servant of God.

083-412-1506

Through the power of the Spirit, the leaders of the Early Church brought Christianity from obscurity to greatness. *Lead to Succeed* will teach you the leadership secrets of these thoroughly dedicated men and women, from John the Baptist to John the Revelator.

083-411-9803

LOOK FOR THEM WHEREVER CHRISTIAN BOOKS ARE SOLD!

BEACON HILL PRESS
OF KANSAS CITY